7 Steps to Sharing Your School's Story on Social Media

7 Steps to Sharing Your School's Story on Social Media empowers school leaders to use social media through a simple and accessible plan that increases engagement and enhances the school's vision and mission. In a step-by-step guide for easy implementation, this book provides the nuts and bolts, as well as the strategic planning necessary, to ensure intentionality and impact of your social media presence. The authors explain how to measure impact and improve your strategies to ensure important information about your school is conveyed accurately, clearly, and effectively. Whether you use the 7 steps in order or you're just looking for some invigorating new ideas or you want to find new ways to connect, collaborate, and share, there is something for every school leader in this book.

Jason Kotch is the principal of Garnet Valley Elementary School in Glen Mills, Pennsylvania, USA.

Edward Cosentino is the principal of Clemens Crossing Elementary School in Columbia, Maryland, USA.

D1496159

Other Eye on Education Books Available from Routledge
(www.routledge.com/eyeoneducation)

7 Steps to Sharing Your School's Story on Social Media

Jason Kotch and Edward Cosentino

Routledge
Taylor & Francis Group

NEW YORK AND LONDON

First published 2018
by Routledge
711 Third Avenue, New York, NY 10017

and by Routledge
2 Park Square, Milton Park, Abingdon, Oxon, OX14 4RN

Routledge is an imprint of the Taylor & Francis Group, an informa business

© 2018 Taylor & Francis

The right of Jason Kotch and Edward Cosentino to be identified as authors of this work has been asserted by them in accordance with sections 77 and 78 of the Copyright, Designs and Patents Act 1988.

Library of Congress Cataloging-in-Publication Data
A catalog record for this book has been requested.

ISBN: 978-1-138-04895-9 (hbk)
ISBN: 978-1-138-04897-3 (pbk)
ISBN: 978-1-315-16987-3 (ebk)

Typeset in Optima
by Sunrise Setting Ltd, Brixham, UK

Dedication

The authors would like to dedicate this book to the following people

From Jason:

To my family who supports me every day in this lifestyle of being a principal, school leader, learner, innovator, and author. My wife, Meghan, encourages me to make the most of every opportunity. My children, Allie, Abigail, and Ryan, inspire me to create a school where every child is treated as part of our family. The unwavering support of my family, no matter my schedule or list of passion projects, drives me every day.

To my parents, Woody and Maria, who raised me through their guidance and care, always allowing me to make my own decisions and to learn from them. It all worked out and I enjoy making them proud. Lauren, Dave, and I appreciate all you do and have done for us.

To my late grandfather, Vito, a superintendent whose heart was larger than life and who showed me how to value all relationships. I'll never forget my summers visiting schools with you: shooting baskets in the gym, stamping new textbooks, stuffing Board packets, and admiring your presence.

To all of the other authors in my family, Gaetana, Alice, Michael, and more, who left a few genes for me to complete this book. I hope you enjoy reading it.

From Edward:

To my family who are my support and have encouraged me to follow my dreams to become a teacher. I was able to be part of a school system that has been such a positive part of my life as a student, a teacher, and an administrator. My wife, Carolyn, who has been by my side all the way.

She has always been reassuring to me and inspired me to take risks and take whatever path I chose in my career. My two daughters, Ellie and Katherine, who are my pride and joy! My parents, Sal and Caroline, who moved to Columbia, Maryland in 1975, a planned community focused on inclusivity and diversity. Who would have ever thought how influential and impactful this area would be on my life? They always supported me along the way, giving me the right balance of guidance and independence.

To the people who had an incredible influence on my education, my career, and my life. My teacher and advisor, Mr. Eric Ebersole, at Wilde Lake High School. My first principal, Mr. Glenn Heisey, who hired me to be a teacher at Hollifield Station Elementary School. His leadership, advice, support, and friendship has helped to define my career as a career of service to students, teachers, parents, and community.

Contents

Meet the Authors

Jason Kotch, @JMKotchEdD, is the principal of Garnet Valley Elementary School in Glen Mills, Pennsylvania. He started his career in Garnet Valley right out of college and has been there ever since. Jason began in education as a fifth grade teacher and then became the school's instructional support teacher before becoming assistant principal. He went on to be the principal of Concord Elementary and then returned to Garnet Valley Elementary as the principal. Jason's passion for school leadership runs throughout his family. A third generation school administrator, Jason has spent his life around schools. He admired his grandfather as he led the Oceanside School District on Long Island as Superintendent of Schools and collaborated with his mother as she guided Media Elementary in the Rose Tree Media School District, in Media, Pennsylvania, as the principal in the same school and district where he earlier attended. Jason's father also went into school leadership later in his career at the University of Pennsylvania School of Dental Medicine after retiring from his private practice. Jason was recognized as a Pennsylvania Keystone Technology Integrator early in his career and has always had an interest in technology. His doctoral dissertation researched the use of interactive whiteboards in the classroom and emphasized the importance of professional learning. At Garnet Valley Elementary, Jason has been able to fulfill his vision of being a collaborative, innovative, and passionate leader through his use of social media in becoming a connected educator and in sharing the impressive accomplishments of the staff and students each day.

Edward Cosentino, @PrincipalECos, is the principal of Clemens Crossing Elementary School in Columbia, Maryland. He has worked for the Howard County Public School System for his entire career. He served as a fourth and fifth grade teacher and an assistant principal before becoming a principal in 2012. He was thrilled to be able to return to the school system where he was a student from kindergarten through twelfth grade. Throughout his career, he has enjoyed learning various ways to harness technology to enhance the quality of education for the students he serves. As an early career principal, he believes it is important to strategically and effectively communicate. With the greater prevalence of instant information through social media, he has been interested in utilizing that medium for school use. Out of his Gallup Top Five Strengths (Harmony, Learner, Disciple, Includer, and Self-Assurance), he is especially proud of being a "learner" and an "includer." Both of those strengths relate to his vision of connecting with people while communicating and sharing his school's story through social media. He constantly loves to learn more about the education field and the people involved in teaching. Additionally, the includer in him wants to share the great story of today's modern school with people who want to follow.

Foreword

In schools around the globe, principals and other educators have increasingly recognized the importance of reaching out to parents and their greater school communities. The world changed for all of us in how we communicate with the arrival of the World Wide Web in 1990.

Having been a school leader for the past 18 years, I myself have worked to harness the capabilities and opportunities of the web, to be able to best communicate outside of the school house.

In 2017, the pull on educators continues, holding them accountable to provide broad communications about their work. Additionally, it has become increasingly evident that using social media and other digital formats is essential to grow and share professionally with colleagues around the world, as we no longer work in isolation.

In this practical and grounded book, principals Jason Kotch and Ed Cosentino share with their readers how to begin the foundational work around school mission and vision and then connect that work to leveraging social media for the benefit of the greater school community and sharing your school's story. The reader is walked through step by step, on how to use social media in promoting the work of the school and connecting with families and educators everywhere. Whether a new or veteran administrator, you will be sure to take practical, step-by-step information from this book and find a way to apply it to your own practice.

Thomas Martellone, @TomMartellone
Educator and Connected Principals Blogger,
connectedprincipals.com
Medford, Massachusetts

Preface

Why this Book Was Written

In the summer of 2014, our authors both traveled to Nashville, Tennessee for the National Association of Elementary School Principals Annual Conference. Ed had attended previous NAESP conferences and this was a first for Jason. While both attended the conference, they never met. However, other connections were made that would start the story of how this book came to be. Jason attended a presentation by Dan Butler (@danpbutler) from Epworth, Iowa. Impressed by how Dan managed leading two elementary schools at the same time, Jason struck up a conversation with Dan following the presentation. During the conversation, Dan encouraged Jason to submit a presentation proposal for conference the following summer.

Jason followed Dan's advice and was accepted to present in Long Beach, California for #NAESP15. Jason and Ed both attended sessions on the first day of the Long Beach conference and noticed that they were picking the same sessions as each other. They started talking about leadership, previous conferences, technology, and being from the East Coast. Jason invited Ed to attend his presentation, 12 Months in S.P.A.C.E. (Strategic Planning Affecting Culture & Environment), the next day. During that presentation, Ed contributed to the conversation, often sharing interesting ideas that related to his school, philosophy, and beliefs. Jason and Ed continued to keep in touch throughout the conference. Before leaving California, Jason encouraged Ed to present next summer as Dan had encouraged him the year before. Instead of submitting separate proposals, the two decided to collaborate throughout the school year and then submit a joint idea. The original thought was to use a different communication tool each month, discuss how it worked, and then document the results for the presentation.

The duo of Jason and Ed never got past Twitter and Facebook. They continued to build their followings in those spaces and never left. When it was time to submit a presentation proposal, the 7 Steps for Sharing Your School's Story were born. The presentation was accepted and presented at National Harbor, Maryland during #NAESP16. While preparing for the presentation, Jason and Ed began communicating with Routledge to write a book for their Eye on Education Series. The book came together over the following school year as Jason and Ed continued connecting with other educators and sharing the stories of the schools on social media.

7 Steps to Sharing Your School's Story on Social Media is a practical guide for school leaders who are interested in communicating with their school communities in methods beyond traditional newsletters. These leaders would include teachers, principals, supervisors, directors, superintendents, and those who might communicate for them such as communications and public relations specialists. The knowledge learned from the *7 Steps* will guide and inspire leaders to create a consistent message for their schools to increase the communication, interaction, and input that enhances leadership of great schools.

Organization of the Book

The advice given throughout the *7 Steps* is intertwined with stories from the elementary schools where Jason and Ed are and have been principals. Most chapters, or steps, start with instructions and ideas for the development of the school leader's social media communication plan. Stories from the authors' schools follow the instructions. The stories are intended to provide examples, gravity to the effectiveness of the step, and inspiration for what using social media looks like in action. The 7 Steps are the heart of the book surrounded by a motivational introduction and thought-provoking conclusion. Each step is titled to be self-explanatory so that the reader can return to the book as a quick reference while the overall plan is put into action. The 7 Steps to Sharing Your School's Story on Social Media are:

Step 1: Connecting Your Vision and Mission to a Social Media Purpose

Step 2: Hashtag It

Step 3: Traditional Methods that Build a Social Media Following

Step 4: Making It Happen

Step 5: Will Anyone Follow Me?

Step 6: Is It Working?

Step 7: What's Next?

The 7 Steps can be read and completed in order or the reader may jump around with the guidance of the authors from time to time. For example, arrival in Step 3 – Traditional Methods that Build a Social Media Following – will find the reader needing to have active social media accounts set up so that the names and handles on the accounts can be publicized. Readers who do not have accounts will want to jump to Step 4 – Making It Happen – to create the account(s) and then return to Step 3. This also shows how the book was designed to be flexible for new, intermediate, and experienced social media users. Step 7 – What's Next? – concludes the 7 Steps with many lists of ideas to expand your social media presence. This chapter is more of a reference for when you need a change, your posts get stale, or you need a solution to delivering your school's message in a certain way.

Special Features

Throughout the book, quotes are called out and highlighted to attract the reader's attention to the book's social media presence. Readers can connect with the authors and other readers to discuss the quotes and collaborate in thought-provoking discussion online using the hashtag, #7StepStories.

The book is also direct and to the point as it was written for busy, practicing school leaders. The lists, reflective questions, and easy-to-navigate format was created for the active professional who seeks new professional learning from many resources and will want to gain an understanding of this book quickly.

Finally, each of the 7 Steps concludes with some "homework" for you, the reader and school leader. Each Step ends with a "School Leaders To Do List" for quick, practical application of the main components explained and shared in each step. Each list recaps what to do next as you put all 7 Steps together to connect, collaborate, and share your school's story on social media.

Acknowledgments

We would like to acknowledge that this book was only possible thanks to the collaboration we enjoy with so many connected educators. Social media is a constant stream of information and we have heard, discussed, and tried many different ideas in our schools over the past four years and also while writing this book. While we couldn't tell you exactly where every idea came from, we acknowledge that this book is the work of many. We are simply the ones who sat down, in many locations, to write it. We hope that everyone reading this book takes pride in their accomplishments in telling their schools' stories and is inspired to continue connecting with the communities influenced by our schools.

We also acknowledge that we are both very fortunate to be able to lead schools in successful and supportive school districts where we are encouraged to build relationships that will further student success. We are grateful to the Garnet Valley School District and Howard County Public School System for their support and for entrusting us with leading our schools. More specifically, we appreciate the staff members of Garnet Valley Elementary School and Clemens Crossing Elementary School. If social media is the vehicle, you are all the drivers and the passengers. We take turns in those collaborative roles as we build schools together that make us so proud.

Finally, we acknowledge that writing this book was something new for us and definitely challenged our fortitude at times. We again thank our wives, Meghan and Carolyn, and our principal colleagues, Tom, Michael, and Keith, for their encouragement and support as we made the most of this opportunity.

Introduction

Imagine a free tool that school administrators can use on a daily basis to help you connect and effectively communicate with your school community. Imagine having the ability to communicate to hundreds of followers at any time of the day with the purpose of sharing the highlights and happenings in a school. Imagine being able to use that tool from your iPhone or any handheld device. Principals and school administrators wear many different hats in the 21st century of school administration and leadership. One of the many different hats is communications director or public information officer. Principals do not have the luxury of having a dedicated person as a public information officer or communications director. That often falls upon the principal or his or her designee. Unlike in the not too distant past, principals have the ability to take control of his or her message when it comes to communicating to their school community.

Effective communication is critical to the success of a school. One of the first things you learn as a leader and school administrator is the importance of strong communication skills. In fact, many principal interviews require a written sample to gauge how well you can write in a short period of time. Whether it is to establish your vision and mission for your school, to publish a weekly newsletter, or to craft a welcome back memo to your school community, communication is an essential skill and requirement for the job. That has been the case way before the digital age of computers, the internet, and social media. Now that we are deep into the social media era, principals and school leaders can strategically and purposefully utilize simple and modern tools to make a major impact on their school and school community.

Imagine having the ability to communicate to hundreds of followers at any time of the day with the purpose of sharing the highlights and happenings in a school. #7StepStories

It wasn't too long ago when communication was simply the weekly paper newsletter that was sent home in a student's "Take-Home" folder. With the advent of email and the greater accessibility of email, paper communication eventually gave way to electronic communication. This happened in society in general and in schools. The ease of sending communication by email made schools "go green." Schools quickly invested in ways to gather email addresses in order to quickly disseminate information from school to home. Fewer and fewer informational papers, newsletters, and flyers, that used to be stuffed in every pocket of a folder, would come home from school. Schools would have new means of disseminating information. This ultimately resulted in a variety of ways to send messages out through email from school. This also included posts and updates periodically on websites. It became time to move beyond the weekly newsletter.

Schools throughout the country are often a few steps behind technology compared with the business world. This is not a fault of the people or the schools. It is simply the fact that schools are governed by school boards who take time to review policy and update it according to the latest trends. Nevertheless, school boards, school systems, and schools often eventually do catch up. This is the case with social media.

Social media is one of the most impactful ways we have communicated in recent years. Social media is not only a way to connect with people through social networking, it is also a place to access information. Social media has transformed society with quick bursts of information, ideas, and opinions to connect people. How did we communicate and connect with each other before social media? In schools, we used a lot of paper! Like newspapers, they often got piled up, often missed, and thrown out with the trash. Now, schools are, or at least should be, taking advantage of technology. Not all school leaders who are responsible for this are digital natives or early adopters so collaboration and support are key in developing their willingness to share school information in digital formats.

When did this social media craze begin? Facebook started in 2004 as an online tool for college students at Harvard. It expanded to the local area and then quickly spread to high schools, post-college people, and shortly after that, the general public. Twitter emerged shortly after Facebook in 2006. Twitter is also a social networking site, but was also classified as a micro-blogging site or an information network. Twitter limited the number of characters in a micro-blog post or tweet to 140. People monitor information or follow other people or organizations on Twitter. At the same time, Apple introduced its smartphone, the iPhone, in 2007. This paved the way for many other companies to have smartphones, tablets, and other devices. With portable technology readily available, people could get information on their mobile devices instantaneously. Technology was moving at a breakneck pace!

It took a while for those social media platforms to make their way into schools, because schools had to figure out how the latest technology could benefit the operations of schools and school systems. It took a while, but recently, school districts around the country updated their policies on the use of social media in their schools. The updating of policies and procedures in schools helped to pave the way for school staff to take advantage of free tools like Twitter and Facebook to engage with their communities using social media.

You may be asking, why use social media in schools? Recently, the Council of Chief State School Officials and the National Policy Board for Educational Administration (2015) revised the standards that guided professional practices of school leaders, the Professional Standards for Educational Leaders (PSEL). Within those professional standards is Standard 8. Standard 8 is defined as:

Standard 8: Meaningful Relationships with Families and Community

Effective educational leaders engage families and the community in meaningful, reciprocal, and mutually beneficial ways to promote each student's academic success and well-being.

c) Engage in regular and open two-way communication with families and the community about the school, students, needs, problems, and accomplishments.

The PSEL standards define the importance of communication in schools. The standards do not dictate how educational leaders must engage and communicate, but it is imperative for school leaders to reflect upon strategies to communicate and communicate well with their school's community.

There are a number of reasons to use social media. More and more parents use and expect to receive their information through their technology in their pockets or purses. Having information at their fingertips is something that this generation of parents who have school-aged children are more accustomed to and comfortable with. It does not mean that schools abandon all other ways of communication, but it does mean that schools and school leaders need to differentiate how they disseminate information. Schools and school leaders should have a clear and public communication plan. Another consideration for schools and school administrators to consider when it comes to social media is the fact that we often only hear the negative implications of social media. People easily hide behind their technology anonymously. With that level of anonymity comes unchecked, hurtful, and hateful content that occupies social media feeds.

KEY TIPS – Reasons to Use Social Media

- Providing parents/guardians with information at their fingertips
- Celebrating our successes
- Quickly disseminating updates and information
- Modeling digital citizenship
- Writing the narrative on public education
- Sharing our school's story

On the other hand, as educators we have the enormous opportunity and greater responsibility to model appropriate use of social media within our school community. The use of social media is a blank canvas for sharing the day-to-day life of a school. We can celebrate successes of our students and staff. We can share important reminders of events and get that information out quickly. We can disseminate information for parents and the community so they can receive notifications on any of their devices. The types of information that can be shared are almost endless. Whether it is a newsletter or current method of teaching, we can share important information for parents to learn what goes on behind the walls of a school. In an age where people hide behind their computers and devices for ill-intentioned reasons, schools can model the positive use of social media by sharing all of the great things going on within your school building.

The use of social media is a blank canvas for sharing the day-to-day life of a school. #7StepStories

We hope you enjoy this book. Over the past three years, we have been testing and trying different strategies to engage with our school communities. We share ideas and experiences in the upcoming chapters from our school communities which have worked well for us. We hope you try them and let us know how it went. The upcoming 7 Steps are a plan to get you started that is strategic in making a successful communication plan using social media. We will refer to these steps throughout the book:

Step 1: Connecting Your Vision and Mission to a Social Media Purpose

Step 2: Hashtag It

Step 3: Traditional Methods that Build a Social Media Following

Step 4: Making It Happen

Step 5: Will Anyone Follow Me?

Step 6: Is It Working?

Step 7: What's Next?

We believe these are seven practical steps to consider when using social media within your school. Each step is also loaded with ideas to implement in your school. Whether you use the 7 Steps in order or simply to get invigorating new ideas, we know that there is something for every school leader in this book. Ultimately, we hope this book is a conduit for us to build a connection between our schools and yours. We are all better when inspiring and supporting each other. As you go, interact with us on Twitter at @7StepStories or on our Facebook Page, 7 Steps to Sharing Your School's Story on Social Media, at @7StepStories.

Step 1 – Connecting Your Vision and Mission to a Social Media Purpose

The first step to using social media is connecting your vision and mission of the school while reflecting on our own experiences that define our leadership style and philosophy. We've all been in a faculty meeting that should have been an email. We've even led those meetings thinking we were doing the right thing. Strategic planning conjures the same thoughts in our minds. Sitting through endless meetings where stakeholders proverbially wrestle over just the right preposition or the perfect adjective to describe our school. Despite our feelings, the initial steps of strategic planning hold a high priority in successfully telling your school's story and it can be an invigorating, uplifting experience as well.

Step 1 – Connecting Your Vision and Mission to a Social Media Purpose – begins your journey through the 7 Steps with a refinement to strategic planning. Once you have identified the vision and mission of your school, you will connect it to a purpose for using social media. This purpose will convey a consistent message to your school's community through the use of many communication platforms. You will solicit and receive feedback on how each of these programs is serving your purpose to further refine your leadership philosophy as you develop a social media communications plan.

Strategic Planning

Initiating a strategic planning process connects your school's direction to the purpose of your social media use. As the first steps are creating a vision and a mission, this will provide your social media followers with focused information on your school. Consistency will be key as you develop more of a following.

To begin this process, we need to start with a growth mindset. Dweck (2006) wrote that a "growth mindset is based on the belief that your basic qualities are things you can cultivate through your efforts" (p. 7). We need to believe that we learn from experience and that we are all able to grow and achieve. Adopting this mindset engages our stakeholders in developing a vision and mission for our school. The definitions of each are best when simplified.

Your mission is what you do, who you do it for, and how you do it. The mission of the Garnet Valley Elementary School (n.d., Vision & Mission) is to "maximize the potential of all students by empowering them to do their personal best." The mission should also be concise so that it can easily be understood, reinforced, and recited when used in a decision making model. Your vision is simply explained as well. Your vision is your north star. It guides your action and plans. It's where you want to be in five, ten, or fifteen years. It's focused on achieving what you can't yet imagine or even picture. It's preparing for what we do not know. "Educating and inspiring respectful, socially responsible learners who use 21st century and critical thinking skills to contribute within local and global societies" is the vision for Garnet Valley Elementary. It was important for Garnet Valley Elementary to include global ideas in its vision as students are now competing in a workforce that is truly international and unlimiting.

Consistency will be key as you develop more of a following. #7StepStories

At Clemens Crossing Elementary School in Howard County, Maryland our school's mission is "to inspire continual achievement by fostering a safe, positive and nurturing environment where learning, teaching and diversity are valued." Our mission has been in place for over ten years under two principals. It continues to embody the culture of our school as a diverse community of learners in a safe academic environment. It not only reflects the makeup of our school, but also helps fulfill the vision of Columbia, Maryland as a whole. Columbia, Maryland, founded in 1967, was committed to build communities focused on eliminating racial, religious, and class barriers. Clemens Crossing Elementary School's mission is an intersection of the planned community vision and the school system's promise of a quality education.

Start with Why

Simon Sinek's "Start with Why" TED Talk (2013) helps to provide focus and inspiration for generating ideas to build a mission and vision. Most schools are part of a larger school district or county system. Often there are already some goal areas or parameters that have been developed at the broader level. Using the goal areas of the district as a guide, the school-level team can identify the why for each area. Garnet Valley School District (garnetvalleyschools.com) in Glen Mills, Pennsylvania, has three goal areas as part of its strategic plan: Student Achievement, Safe and Caring Environment, and Management of Systems. Student achievement focuses on curriculum, teaching and learning, and professional learning. Safe and Caring Environment emphasizes the social and emotional learning of the students, while Management of Systems is effective use of resources, communication, and fiscal responsibility.

The Howard County Public School System's (2013) vision is simple and succinct, "Every student is **inspired** to learn and **empowered** to excel." The four pillars of the school system's goals are: Goal 1: Students; Goal 2: Staff; Goal 3: Families; Goal 4: Organization.

Vision and Mission

After viewing and discussing Sinek's TED Talk, the Garnet Valley Elementary faculty defined its "why" for each of the three strategic areas. This was completed individually and in groups to muster ideas at many different levels. The ideas were then marked as either vision or mission material. Words were chosen from the various surveys to narrow down ideas for each. The School Planning team, a group of school leaders, worked through these statements as a group along with gathering input from their respective grade levels and departments. They chose statements generated under each goal area that represented what they wanted to include in the vision and mission. Once the ideas were agreed upon, draft statements were created. After each meeting, the group gave the drafts a few weeks to resonate with the team members. Eventually, drafts of both the vision and mission were created. Mission was completed first as it was easier to focus on the present before defining a direction to achieve future goals in a vision. The drafts were then presented to the school's League for Educational Advancement (LEA). The LEA team comprises parent, community, teacher, administrator,

3

and support staff representatives. The representatives from each of these groups helped to refine the final vision and mission statements.

Examples from the original belief statements based on the purpose for each part of the strategic plan included:

- Students working to their full potential
- Students engaged in learning
- Creating productive community members who believe in social progress
- Preparing students for their futures
- Recognizing individual and group success and progress through personal growth
- Implementing a high-quality curriculum that maximizes technology for critical thinking, digital responsibility, and global citizenship
- Maintaining a safe environment where students can focus and desire to attend school each day
- Valuing social, emotional, and academic growth
- Considering all who are associated with the school and wanting them to feel cared for and appreciated

From these beliefs, the drafted vision statement was then reviewed through the lens of "If we reach our vision, will our students be ready for college and beyond?" After considering this statement, additional thoughts were brainstormed to consider adding:

- Confident learners
- Growth mindset
- 21st century learners
- Individual responsibility and accountability

Garnet Valley Elementary's drafted mission statement also received further review as the team wanted to make it more unique to their school. The strengths of the school that the team discussed started bringing the mission statement to life:

- Pride in the community
- Success being different for each child
- Empowering students to think for themselves
- A school with a unique configuration serving students in grades 3 through 5
- Educating the whole child including successful programs in music and the arts
- Cultivating uniqueness
- Cohesive support of staff and parents/guardians
- Dedicated staff
- Opportunities to be creative in designing and implementing learning activities
- Administrative priorities rooted in supporting students' needs

The vision and mission statements gained clarity as the drafts moved from generally good principles in education to unique strengths of the school. Soon after, the vision and mission statements were adopted and began to be publicized and relied upon when making decisions and plans for the growth of the school community.

KEY TIPS – Drafting Vision and Mission Statements

- Define your vision as where you want to be in five, ten, or fifteen years
- Define your mission as what you do, who you do it for, and how you do it
- Seek input on the core values and beliefs for your organization
- Define your "why"
- Separate ideas into category by vision or mission
- Draft statements, share them, and improve them
- Assure that your vision and mission are unique to your school!

A typical strategic planning process would now move on from vision and mission to goals, objectives, measurement tools, and feedback loops. However, now that we have briefly reviewed how to develop the vision and mission, the journey through our 7 Steps begins to turn towards social media. Starting to incorporate social media into your school's publicity requires attention and focus. It's best done in purposeful ways. When parents and guardians know the expectations for social media, they know where to find what they are looking to find and also encounter what you, as the school leader, want to emphasize.

So, after all of the time and effort developing new vision and mission statements, it's time to show them off and use social media to share all of the good things going on in your school and eventually move to interacting with parents in more than traditional ways. Leading a school is finding a balance between the school reflecting the community and creating an environment where the education in our schools pushes the community farther. Social media shares the drive that our schools possess to continually learn and grow within our schools and out into our communities.

Leading a school is finding a balance between the school reflecting the community and creating an environment where the education in our schools pushes the community farther. #7StepStories

Connecting to Your Social Media Purpose

At this point, in Step 1, we are developing a frame of reference and purpose for using social media. Connecting to your mission, think about what you can post that reflects what you do, who you do it for, and how you do it. Even if you aren't set up on a platform yet, you can start to list ideas. Set goals for yourself:

- How often will I post?
- What will I include?
- Do the activities we do reflect our vision and/or mission?

- Are we providing experiences that empower students to be the central tendency of our classrooms?
- Are we as student-centered as we desire?

Posting during or after special events is a great way to start. It also provides reflection on the learning activities we plan for and provide in our schools. Looking at your ideas and posts will help you deliver on the mission that your stakeholders created as you begin to connect with parents. Once parents start to understand the daily activities in school then your social media purpose will shift as your school also begins to shift from mission to vision. Making this shift is extremely exciting!

Once your mission is firmly established, it will lead to substantial work on the systems that affect daily life in a school: scheduling, staffing, job assignment, building culture, recognizing achievements in process and product, and resource allocation. Revising all of these systems through the lens of your vision is hard work but it's good work and it strengthens your school for students. You will be sharing more with parents than you ever have before. It doesn't take long before your social media presence far exceeds what had traditionally been gleaned through a weekly newsletter and occasional visits to the school.

Your mission is getting closer to being cemented, for now, as strategic planning is an ongoing process that will bring you back to the beginning again eventually. Crafting a mission, aligning it to your school, changing mindset to embrace it, and sharing the work that brings it to life takes time. Many schools will take a few years to get to this point. You will know you are there when you are making minor adjustments to the major systems each year instead of managing major overhauls. When you and your school are ready, it's time to shift from an emphasis on your mission to delivering on your vision. Step 4 – Making It Happen – will provide more specific ideas about what to post to help you establish your mission and prepare for your vision.

In many ways, establishing your mission statement and delivering it to your school community sets a foundation for visionary work. Moving towards your vision is invigorating and challenging. It's moving from a stable environment to one that pushes expectations, takes risks, and promotes teachers as leaders. While your social media presence may start with just the school leader, it will eventually expand so that the staff is creating content as well. The shift in your school from mission work to vision work will be the same as your growth on social media. You will start posting about your school story and eventually use social media to connect with others who share the same vision. Social media transforms the connections you have to others. You will be able to form partnerships, contact experts, research in real time, and solve problems with a global impact. All of this occurs from shifting your emphasis from our daily work to our future goals. It's a process that starts with developing the core values of your school, using social media to share them, and then expanding your social media impact to prepare students for a future they are yet to fully understand.

Moving towards your vision is invigorating and challenging. #7StepStories

The Purpose of Each Platform

As we define the "why" and identify a purpose for what we do in school, we also need to make some decisions about the purpose of our social media use. The connection to delivering your vision and mission to the families that support your students is hopefully clear but there are more decisions to be made. It's recommended to start with a very clearly communicated purpose so that parents and guardians know what to expect and when it will be delivered. As your purpose evolves, communication to families should be updated as well. One way to do this is to post on your website the social media platforms you will be using, why you are using them, and how they will be used. Policies on social media use vary so be sure to check with your district or school system before embarking on this journey. More on policy is in Step 4 – Making It Happen.

As you get familiar with the different platforms, you will find strengths in each of them. Some are easier to monitor comments if you are concerned with doing that. Others do not verify email addresses and can make it difficult to be aware of who is viewing your content. Many of the platforms can also be linked together so posts in one place can apply on different platforms. We all use other communication tools as well so you need to consider how they all are going to relate when you are putting together a communication plan for updating parents and eventually engaging them in providing meaningful feedback for your school. Here is one school's example (www.garnetvalleyschools.com/gves) of how different tools are used:

Facebook: Facebook has been found to be the preferred platform of the parents of elementary school-age students. We use Facebook to share pictures and videos of special things that happen in our school. Please share our posts to show how our school is empowering students to reach their maximum potential. Most posts to Facebook come directly from our Twitter Feed. Be sure to "like" and "follow" us on Facebook.

Twitter: Twitter is the universal platform in our district that connects all of our schools. Follow us on Twitter and also see what our other schools are posting. Our Facebook posts mostly originate here. Twitter is used by more parents as their children get into the secondary schools. Since the secondary schools use Twitter to connect with their students, more secondary parents are also on Twitter. Be sure to "follow" us and be sure to retweet the amazing things occurring in our school.

Instagram: Instagram is used by most students as they get older. Many parents are also using Instagram for personal use. We have some posts now on Instagram as well. Posts that originate on Instagram will also be seen on Twitter and Facebook. Instagram will post a link on Twitter to the Instagram post. On Facebook, the original Instagram post is able to be seen. Since Instagram only allows posting directly through its app, posts that originate on Twitter or Facebook will not be on Instagram. We occasionally post on Instagram for our Instagram users but do not use it as much since the connections to the other platforms are not seamless. Hopefully, we will be adding Instagram Stories for you in the future.

Remind: Remind is a text messaging service that parents/guardians can subscribe to. Remind is mostly used by us to send reminders about spirit days and special events. Since Remind text messaging goes right to your mobile device, it is an effective way for us to connect with you. However, we use it sparingly to not overwhelm parents with text messages where notifications are instantaneous.

Website: Our website includes information about our school, our parent organization, and connections to our district. It is also where you register for our email e-alerts. E-alerts are the most common messaging system in our district. E-alerts are where you will initially receive important information, weekly announcements, and school closing information. School closing information is posted by our school district on district social media sites but is not posted on our school social media. Please rely on our e-alerts, website, and district-level communication for all school closing information.

Email and phone: When in doubt, please call our office at the main number. A directory of staff email addresses is also on our website. Please do not send urgent information by email. Dismissal changes or other urgent matters should be called in to the school so that you have a confirmation when they are received.

The example above is found on the front page of the school's website and published each week in the weekly announcements. What does it accomplish? It shows parents that there are options. It shows how the posts are created and it explains what not to expect. Frequent social media users will expect more. Since communication in schools is a matter of student safety, we need parents to understand where they will find important information. It is beneficial to be clear that more traditional methods are still available and that they should not rely on social media for everything.

For most schools, it is the principal leading the way with communication so only so much can be shared in this method. However, you will find that your purposes will expand as you gain more followers, become more comfortable with posting, and look for ways to make your social media use interactive. As you do so, it will be important to provide professional learning around creating teacher accounts. The teacher accounts will also need to be public for the school leader to be able to retweet and share the posts from teachers within the school. Teachers will need to be informed of confidentiality rules such as not posting a student's picture and his or her name in the same post. While we want to share our story, we also need to follow best practices for internet safety and be aware of students whose parents have opted them out of being photographed or recorded.

KEY TIPS – Choosing Social Media Platforms

- Facebook – most popular with elementary school parents/guardians

- Twitter – most convenient for connecting with other schools

- Instagram – students have been there for a while and parents are moving there next

- Instagram will post nicely on Facebook when linked

- Twitter will post to Facebook so Facebook users can see your Twitter pictures

- You cannot use a third-party app to post on Instagram

Listening to Your Parents

You will quickly become inspired to do even more on social media as you begin to get feedback from parents. It is very common for a parent to ask us, "Who does all your posting?" or "Who do you have run your social media?" Parents are sometimes surprised that we make the time to do it but we do because we value it so much. At a recent school event, a parent was casually talking about how he mostly uses Twitter for news and current events. He shared that the posts he gets from school are always positive and uplifting. Quite frankly, he looked forward to the school's posts because they are a needed break from often upsetting news being continually reported in the social media stream about discouraging current events. This also helps illustrate the positivity in schools and hopefully model appropriate social media behavior.

We've made some generalizations about parents' social media use. Elementary parents tend to start on Facebook. Secondary parents join their children on Twitter and Instagram. Obviously, there are many more communication apps such as SnapChat, WhatsApp, Google$^+$, and more. Schools can't cover them all so they tend to use apps that provide a public forum where posts go to many people at once. To determine the best platform for your school, your best bet is to ask by surveying your stakeholders. Sometimes these decisions may be made for you by school leaders above you, but if not be sure to query your parents. Google Forms and Survey Monkey are two common tools for free surveys. Ask your parents what platforms they use, how often they use them, how often they would like school information, and what media they prefer. Most parents are still preferring pictures and text; however, students would rather watch a video. (Think YouTube channel.)

Knowing the preferences and social media platforms of your parents will help to tailor your purpose and set up your tools. Step 6 – Is It Working? – will provide detailed information for analyzing your social media use and the connections you make with it. But, again, we are just at the beginning. You will get there! For now, ask and see what information you get. Start with that and provide parents the best match to their requests. Then, as your presence grows, you can start to work in different types of posts. Ask your students what to post next. They will suggest different ideas like video, 360 degree pictures, photo filters, and trends before parents do. Popular trends on social media recently have included the #mannequin-challenge (the White House under former president Obama got in on this one) or using the #boomerang feature on Instagram.

KEY TIPS – What Students Enjoy

- Selfies
- Going live
- Stories made with filters
- Boomerang
- Latest trends like water bottle flipping, fidget spinners, or popular songs and dances

---

You can always find more trends on Twitter through the Explore button. And, of course, don't forget to embrace the #selfie. Students love to take and be in selfies! We don't carry around selfie sticks but there are tools like a selfie stick, flexible tripod, or smartwatch app that can help you if you don't have long arms for snapping a good selfie! Attaching your phone to a flexible tripod and then activating the shutter through an app on your watch will give you many different angles and views for your pictures. You will need to hone your photography skills and be sure to post pictures that your audience will enjoy and the people in your pictures will appreciate.

Don't forget to embrace the #selfie. #7StepStories

Connecting your vision and mission to your social media purpose takes several steps. Some basic strategic planning can get your vision and mission in place. Defining your social media purpose will depend on school policies and the effect you want to have. This will all evolve over time. Your social media presence will begin as a one-way communication with parents before shifting to being more interactive. Be overt about how you are using social media. You want parents to know more about your school and also don't want them to miss anything important that is sent through traditional methods like your website or email. Include parents and students in planning your overall presence and also in your posts. Sharing your school's story on social media is "social." It's something we do together. Before you move onto Step 2 – Hashtag It – here's your homework:

Step 1 – School Leaders To Do List

1. Strategic planning to collaboratively develop your school's vision and mission

2. Share, share, share – share your vision and mission work and final products

3. Set your purpose for using social media (you don't need to pick your platforms yet)

4. Use your mission as the foundation for your work while planning to transcend to your vision once the foundation is stable

5. Gather input from parents and students about social media use and preferences.

Step 2 – Hashtag It

In Step 1 – Connecting Your Vision and Mission to a Social Media Purpose – we developed a renewed vision and mission for your school, if needed. We then created a communication plan to let your students and parents know that we will be using social media to tell our school's story. Finally, we started some research on what platforms are being used. Now, it's time to continue our planning by creating a hashtag (#) for your school.

Your school's hashtag will be the common thread that connects all posts on social media to your school. Users will add your hashtag to each of their posts to make their posts searchable by the username and also by the hashtag. This allows any social media user to search for your hashtag and find anything posted with the hashtag attached to the post. Hashtags are how social media users find "trends" and join conversations on the same topic. "Trends" are when many people are posting using the same hashtag. What's trending is measured on sites in different ways and there is usually a quick way to find trending hashtags.

With a hashtag, everything using the hashtag is linked together so you do not need to follow or be friends with any of the users in the thread when their accounts are public. It joins the online community together to connect and is also a powerful tool in education. Creating your school's unique hashtag is the next step in preparing your social media presence and is one that is most fun when your school is involved in created it.

Establishing Your Vision and Mission

We started this social media plan with creating a vision and mission first so that you can use either when creating a hashtag for your school.

Many schools will use their school name, mascot name, or some other identifiable information in their hashtag. Hashtags like this are often created by one person, most likely the person who heads the social media accounts used for the school. Some districts may suggest or assign district and school hashtags. Another way to create a hashtag is to involve the students. To do this, you first share the school's vision and mission. This can be done in many ways.

The vision and mission can be part of your opening assemblies at the beginning of the year, they can be part of any speeches or communications you send to parents and students, and they can be posted around your school. You should also refer to your school's vision and mission when making decisions. Purposeful and timely use of the vision and mission will reinforce its value to your school community. After students get to know the vision and mission, the students can be asked to choose the keywords in each. The keywords can then be combined with any identifiable information from your school. Students, by class, can create a hashtag to be considered for the school. Once all classes get to suggest a possible hashtag, the school can vote on the different contenders. Google Surveys are our go-to again for getting this type of feedback. Tally the votes, see which hashtag has the most, and then check into your new hashtag before announcing the winner. Don't get too excited before doing your research on the possible hashtag. You want it to be special for your school so that it can serve the purpose of connecting everyone interacting with your accounts.

Purposeful and timely use of the vision and mission will reinforce its value to your school community. #7StepStories

Your One and Only Hashtag

It's important that your hashtag is unique. To find out if it is, you will want to search the possible hashtag for your school on any social media platform you plan to use. For us, we mostly use Twitter and Facebook. However, checking Instagram would be a good idea too. If your hashtag is something generic, someone else may be using it. And it doesn't have to just be another school using it, it can be anyone on social media using it. When the same hashtag is used in different scenarios, search results will show posts outside of your intended audience.

Search results will show users who post with a hashtag. The results will also show top posts, most recent posts, photos, and videos along with an option for viewing everything posted on the hashtag. Check them all before making this big decision! As a non-example, using #bestschool for your hashtag probably wouldn't work. Hopefully, we either think our school is the best or we are working toward it being the best but that doesn't work on social media. How many people do you think have posted something and then used #bestschool? There are a lot of alumni out there who probably think their school is the best. Just a quick search of Twitter for #bestschool finds many schools posting with that hashtag, parents posting proud moments with #bestschool, and students even using it sarcastically. (One student posted a sarcastic comment about getting her phone taken away, in college, and added #bestschool to the post.)

Additionally, hashtags are not case sensitive. Clemens Crossing Elementary thought it was using the creative and unique hashtag #suCCESs. Unfortunately, in the world of Twitter, #suCCESs was connected to anyone else who used the hashtag #success. Another word of caution is to maintain a hashtag that is not too long. The hashtag #jaguarmax is short, succinct, and identifiable with Garnet Valley Elementary School. Another word of caution is to use hashtags for their intended purpose. Many people decided to jumble sentences together with the pound sign in front of it and call that a tweet. It's not! It's hard to read, and it will turn your audience off. That is fine to do on your personal account, but when you are representing your school, your communication plan, and a level of professionalism that you want to portray, we recommend not engaging in that type of practice. #werecommendnotengaginginthistypeoftweeting.

If you want to figure out if a hashtag is used, you can simply type in the hashtag into the search section of Twitter. This will provide you with a list of "top" uses or "latest" uses of that hashtag. If no result shows up, then that hashtag or combinations of characters might not be being used within Twitter. Another way you can help develop a hashtag is through the website ritetag.com. This site allows you to type in any hashtag to determine if the hashtag is in use. For popular hashtags, it will give you information about how those hashtags are connected to other users on Twitter. If you look up #jaguarmax, you will be able to see other accounts associated with this hashtag, and you will be able to see that it is connected to Garnet Valley Elementary School. If you type in #suCCESs, you will find pages of results. This tells us that too many people use that hashtag, and we would not be selecting a unique hashtag for the Clemens Crossing Twitter feed. When you type in #ClemensCougars, no results show up. This tells us no one is using this hashtag. When you type in #CelebrateCCES, nothing shows up either. If we were to use this hashtag, there could be another CCES group out there who might use this as a hashtag. No matter what you decide, this is a great opportunity to be creative. Take advantage of this opportunity and have fun with the selection of part of your Twitter identity.

Make Your Hashtag Yours

Once you choose a hashtag that doesn't return any search results you will want to lock down that hashtag as much as possible. Locking down your hashtag means that you want to start using it and also opening accounts with the hashtag as the username on the account. Hashtags can't be copyrighted or reserved for your use on any of the sites. Anyone can use them but do what you can to establish that it is yours. You will want to get your new hashtag out there in many ways so that when others search for a hashtag to use, they will see you are using the unique one chosen for your school.

Creating accounts using the hashtag also helps to stop others from finding interest in your hashtag and stops students from opening accounts using what your school is reserving for sharing the positive things in your school. It is also very possible that someone will use the hashtag incorrectly at some point. Instead of posting with the hashtag, someone might post using the @ sign. The @ sign, or the Twitter handle, is used to tag a user in a post. The tag notifies the user that you mentioned their account and also provides a link from your post to that account. So, if someone has an account named with your hashtag then they will get a notification of the post. You will also want to put your hashtag in your profile when you set up your accounts. You would include this in the accounts with the hashtag as the name (even though you won't actually use those accounts) and also in your school account that you will set up with your school's name and whatever username you prefer for your school.

KEY TIPS – Your Hashtag

- Collaboratively choose a hashtag to reflect your vision and mission
- Search all platforms for your hashtag to ensure no one else is using it
- Create accounts on all platforms and put your hashtag in your bio
- Open additional "ghost" accounts with your hashtag as the name and handle for the account (You won't actually use these accounts)
- Start posting with your hashtag right away
- Periodically search for your hashtag and review all posts to see how it is being used
- Get ready to promote your hashtag

Putting the hashtag in your profile will direct anyone who searches for that hashtag to your account. Also, starting to post using your hashtag will get posts out there for others to see. You can even post something as simple as, "Our school is now using this hashtag – #numberoneschool." You should also add your new hashtag to your website, letterhead stationery, and signatures on email correspondence. All of these steps help to make your hashtags yours as much as possible and make it unique to your school. The Twitter profile for Garnet Valley Elementary School includes the school motto, "A Caring Community of Learners," and the hashtag, "#jaguarmax."

Garnet Valley Elementary School has been using #jaguarmax for the past two years. This hashtag was created by taking the school district's mascot, the jaguar, and combining it with the idea in the mission statement of "empowering students to reach their **max**imum potential." Students voted for this hashtag over other options when choosing a theme for an upcoming school year. Each year, the school picks a new theme in the spring and students have a chance to design a t-shirt for the theme. The t-shirt is then worn on school spirit days, during school-wide activities like bullying prevention assemblies, to identify students on field trips, and then on field day. This theme was selected when hashtags were getting very popular. #jaguarmax was originally chosen as the school's theme as hashtags were trending in pop culture. It then became the school's hashtag as well once social media began being used to share school information. The hashtag quickly caught on and also became the name of the school's Positive Behavioral Interventions and Supports (PBIS) program.

Innovative Programs to Hashtag

The PBIS program at Garnet Valley Elementary is based on six themes. The themes were chosen to represent skills and character traits that students will need to be successful in the global economy of the 21st century. The skills, connected to the school's vision statement, are dedication, altruism, collaboration, creative thinking, leadership, and perseverance. Each month, students are selected to be recognized for each theme. Garnet Valley Elementary has students in grades three, four, and five. The third grade #jaguarmax program is a little different from the fourth and fifth grade programs. The students recognized in third grade participate in a monthly assembly where their parents, guardians, and family members are invited into the school to see them receive their certificates. Every student in third grade is recognized for one of the themes at some point during the year. The third grade program is run this way for two reasons.

First, the assemblies are held so that the parents of the new third grade students get a chance to visit the school. Second, each student is recognized so that they learn all of the themes in the first year they are being recognized. The assemblies consist of saying the Pledge of Allegiance together, opening comments from the principal, presentations from one or two classes each month about something they are doing in their classroom, certificate presentations where the teachers read the names and shake the students' hands, and then everyone singing the school song. At the end, students who received a certificate and have a special guest at the assembly have a chance to take pictures. Many of these pictures are taken in front of an 8′ × 10′ step and repeat banner covered with #jaguarmax that was ordered online.

The fourth and fifth grade students are presented with their certificates in their homerooms by the school leaders. Each month, two students (along with a few extras at times) are chosen to be recognized for each theme. Fourth and fifth grade is a little more competitive as every student does not receive a certificate. Every student can, however, earn raffle tickets for every theme. Once the students in grades three, four, and five are recognized for the month's theme then the school continues working on that theme for the rest of the month. Students "caught" demonstrating the positive characteristics of the theme receive a raffle ticket. They write their names on the raffle tickets and then send them to the office. The tickets are placed in bingo-board-like pocket holders on a #jaguarmax board outside of the office. Each month winning tickets are picked. The students then select a prize. The prizes range from a snack in the cafeteria for the student, to a #jaguarmax t-shirt, to a pizza party for the student's entire class. Throughout this program, students are reinforced for the positive behaviors while reinforcing the school's hashtag.

Using #jaguarmax as the name of the PBIS system has promoted its use throughout the community. Searches for #jaguarmax now connect social media users to more than just posts from the school. In the spring of 2016, Garnet Valley Elementary started doing an annual school-wide Genius Hour. You can learn a lot about Genius Hour by searching #GeniusHour on Twitter and from A.J. Juliani's book, *Inquiry and Innovation in the Classroom* (Juliani, 2014).

Genius Hour

Genius Hour is based on Google 20% time where students (or Google employees) get to spend part of their regularly scheduled day researching and creating projects based on their interests. Genius Hour has been used as the final rotation of the intervention schedule for the year. Students get to choose research projects based on their interests and passions and then create a product or solution related to their research question. The teachers guide the students to choose projects that can be completed within the allotted number of days and can be constructed with materials available to them at school or at home.

At Garnet Valley Elementary, a student did his Genius Hour on the sandbox video game Minecraft. He then took his project and presented it at a Minecraft conference. His mother tweeted a picture of him from the conference and used #jaguarmax in the picture. This was how the school found out about his presentation at the conference. Once aware of it, one of the school district's instructional technology coaches interviewed the student and wrote a blog about how he turned his Genius Hour project into a Minecraft presentation. The student also later presented the project to the district's Board of School Directors' Education Committee along with another student with whom he had designed a Minecraft website. None of these connections would have been made without the parents posting with the school's hashtag. Connections like this make the hashtag for your school a powerful tool so you really want something unique where your posts and the posts of others intended for your school community don't get lost in a thread with irrelevant posts.

None of these connections would have been made without the parents posting with the school's hashtag. #7StepStories

Social Media Contests

Contests are also an engaging way to spread the use of your hashtag. Contests on social media can occur with or without a lot of planning. Communicating on social media is instantaneous so announcing a contest can spread the word quickly. For those who live in snowy regions, a snow day contest is always entertaining. Simply sending out an idea for parents to post pictures of their children playing in the snow with the school hashtag can get conversations started. Once parents start posting then others start searching for the hashtag to see what pictures are there. Throw in a few prizes once the snow melts and school resumes and the hashtag for your school has spread.

Many contest entries could work by parents posting the results with the school hashtag. Contests over breaks are a means to keep students engaged. Many have advocated for less homework so that students have more time to be innovative. Innovation has found its way into classrooms not just through technology and activities like Genius Hour but also through flexible seating in the classroom. We realize that the desks our students sit in today haven't changed a whole lot. Maybe some of the materials are different but the overall shape and function of a desk has remained the same. Schools are starting to offer students more options in seating and starting to purchase seating that better fosters collaboration, flexibility, and innovation. However, what do we do with all of the traditional desks and chairs that we have?

An idea for an innovative contest is to give students a chance to design and then build a more flexible, functional desk starting with the desks we already have. Imagine what could happen when students and parents work together over a break to redesign a desk that could be in a classroom within weeks. They post their ideas, plans, and results using the school hashtag, get some feedback, make some changes, and then the school picks a few designs to build. The whole project supports innovation, design thinking, social media collaboration on the hashtag, and results in a better learning experience for the student. Most school leaders would be happy to give a few students desks to build once they had seen the plans. Picture a desk covered in whiteboard paint with adjustable height for sitting or standing on rollers for collaboration and storage compartments for an iPad, battery back-up, and other supplies. One of our students could build that and make it ten times better than just the initial ideas. Contests like this that get our students and parents thinking out of the box are the perfect match for partnering with social media. And pulling it all together is the unique school hashtag that anyone can search for and find connections to your school.

KEY TIPS – Uses for Your Hashtag

- Naming your PBIS program
- Promoting student passion projects through Genius Hour
- Snow day contest to share pictures
- Innovation projects like Desk Design Challenges
- Connecting to events in your community
- Collaborating with your social media followers

Creating your school's hashtag is a collaborative experience. #7StepStories

Be Collaborative

Creating your school's hashtag is a collaborative experience. It grows out of your strategic planning work on the vision and mission of your school.

Students can be involved in brainstorming ideas for the hashtag and then also in voting on the final choice. Be sure that your hashtag is unique before you decide to use it. Once you choose it, register accounts across all social media platforms that you will use to help preserve it. Also, list your hashtag in the profile on your school accounts. Using the hashtag as part of your Positive Behavioral Interventions and Supports program will spread the awareness of being able to search social media for your school's story by using the hashtag. Fun (weather-related) and innovative contests are other ways to make more students and parents aware of the school's hashtag. Now that your hashtag is solidified, our next Step will be to publicize all of your communication methods, highlighting your hashtag. But first, your homework from Step 2 – Hashtag It – is:

Step 2 – School Leaders To Do List

1. Start with keywords from your vision and mission to draft hashtag ideas

2. Include students in creating and voting on hashtags

3. Find a unique hashtag for your school and lock it down

4. Relate your hashtag to other programs in your school, like PBIS

5. Run contests using your school hashtag once your social media presence is ready.

Step 3 – Traditional Methods that Build a Social Media Following

In Step 2 – Hashtag It – we discussed the ways to build energy around your social media identity by using a unique hashtag. This chapter – Step 3 – will focus on building your following through traditional methods. Building a following is essential in order to have a successful social media platform. You will need your chosen social media accounts set up at this point but you don't need to be active on them yet. If you don't have accounts previously in use, jump to Step 4 – Making It Happen – to set up your accounts and then come back here.

Formative Assessment

In the classroom, we use formative assessment to determine where our students are and then to create learning paths from there. We are always sure to meet our students where they are to begin building. Let's build our social media following the same way. As the school leader, you are also likely to be the lead communicator. Ask yourself these questions about your current communications plan:

- What methods do we currently use to communicate with our families?
- Where do parents go for school information?
- How do we send routine information?
- What do we do to notify parents/guardians with more urgent information?
- When do we have the opportunity to connect face-to-face?

- Do we promote our school?

- What activities raise school spirit?

- Do we have relationships with local news sources, agencies, and organizations?

- How have we trained parents to use our current communications systems?

Answering these questions will help you meet parents where they are. These are the systems they already know and should be comfortable using. So, we want to use our current methods from the answers to the questions above to direct our stakeholders to our social media presence.

Communication Methods

Let's start with posting our social media profiles in some obvious places. First, your website. You can do a few different things here. The most interesting is adding your Twitter feed right to your homepage. This will create a column on your website for anyone to see your tweets without needing to be logged in to Twitter. It will also help advertise your Twitter presence to anyone on your website. Adding your Twitter feed is easier than you would think. You simply log in to Twitter, go to your setting, and then to widgets. Once you create a widget for your Twitter timeline, you just need to copy the code for the widget and paste it into the editor for your website. Twitter even creates a preview of the timeline for you to see before copying the code. Simple boxes will guide you in the setup so don't worry if you don't understand any coding. Placing a Facebook "Like" button on your website also makes it easy for parents to "Like" your page while on your website and without needing to go to Facebook and look for your Facebook page. To create your customized button, go to developers.facebook.com/docs/plugins/like-button. This site will create the plugins that you want to put on your website to connect with Facebook. It works the same as the Twitter widgets. Just create what you want and then copy and paste it into your website editor. For other sites, like Instagram, you can save an image of the logo and then make the image a link when uploading the image to your website.

KEY TIPS – Website Development

- Place a Facebook "Like" button on the homepage of your website
- Use a widget to put your Twitter feed on the front of your website
- Insert links to any other platforms such as Instagram by using the site logo as a link
- Create a headlining article explaining how your communication tools are used
- Use Storify to archive your social media journey on your website for those not on social media yet

---

Schools send plenty of email so let's be sure that your social media information is on your email template. You will notice in several parts of this 7 Step plan that consistency is key. A consistent email template also directs parents to your social media. Parents will start using different sites at different times so you want to be sure they see your profiles often. A recommended email template might have the name of your school at the top, followed by the school slogan, and hashtag. At the bottom of the template, you can add links or pictures that are linked for all of your social media platforms depending on the service you use to deliver mass emails. Here is the template used at Garnet Valley Elementary:

GARNET VALLEY ELEMENTARY SCHOOL
"A Caring Community of Learners"
#jaguarmax
Body of email
www.garnetvalleyschools.com/gves
www.twitter.com/GarnetValleyES
www.facebook.com/GarnetValleyES
www.instagram.com/GarnetValleyES
www.remind.com/join/jaguarmax

You'll notice that the same name is used on the three social media platforms that this school uses and that the school's hashtag is used for the text messaging service, Remind. Of course, we send individual emails as well.

You can add your hashtag to your email signature, too. Many resources will also have their own buttons built in to make it easier for your stakeholders to connect with your social media platforms. For example, Clemens Crossing and Garnet Valley Elementary schools both use smore.com to develop and disseminate weekly announcements by creating the newsletters on this site. Part of the Smore template includes a place where you can connect links to the various social media platforms to make the connection very easy. This allows you to constantly promote the availability and use of any of your social media sites within each newsletter. For more on Smore and other tools, check out Step 7 – "What's Next?"

Face-to-Face

There are several big events each year where most schools see their students' parents face-to-face. These are opportunities to see many people and to make a personal connection with your social media. These events begin with open houses to start the year followed by Back to School Nights. After that, we have parent/teacher conferences twice a year, the big annual fundraisers, and other events that attract a crowd like movie or bingo nights. Students will love seeing their pictures on social media and many younger students will see them through their parents' accounts.

So, it is important to connect these face-to-face meetings with your social media. You can do this by handing out items with your social media information or with your hashtag. A quick postcard made on a site like vistaprint.com can spread the word. Each year, you can make a new postcard with any theme for the year along with information about connecting with your social media. This is also a great way to remind parents of your school's vision and mission and to also share frequently used information like the attendance line phone number or the school's email address. If you order extra postcards at the beginning of the year, you are sure to find other times to use them like parent conferences or when you start transition meetings for upcoming classes.

Also, as we mentioned in Step 2 – Hashtag It – the photo booth with your hashtag in a repeating pattern is a fun thing to have around during face-to-face events. Like the postcards, the photo booth is something you will use over and over again. Encouraging everyone to take selfies and group pictures at your events spreads the hashtag that works over various platforms. Students being recognized through your PBIS program can have their pictures taken in front of the banner so you can share their accomplishments.

Encouraging everyone to take selfies and group pictures at your events spreads the hashtag that works over various platforms. #7StepStories

School Spirit

While the fundamental purpose of education is to create educated citizens, we see our school goals always being focused on student achievement. We know that students learn more when they are invested, motivated, and proud of their schools. We also know that parent engagement is a key to a successful school. For all of these reasons, we need to promote our schools. Promoting our schools is not a self-promotion, it is a way to increase student achievement and enhance the students' connection to their schools. As we tell our school story on social media, we want to use traditional promotion devices to channel parents to our social media. Here are examples:

T-shirts

No brainer here, right? We make a t-shirt for everything. Just keep in mind ways to involve students in your designs. Some schools make an annual t-shirt. This shirt can be based on a yearly theme and a student design contest can be held to create the design. Be sure to include your hashtag in the design! In elementary school, the annual shirt can be used to show unity against bullying, to identify your students on field trips, and for school spirit during field days and other special events. Making a different, unique shirt with your hashtag in a limited quantity also gives them a special twist. These shirts can be used to recognize staff and students who achieve a special accomplishment. For the rest of your spirit wear, check in with your parent organizations about including your hashtag in their designs.

Giveaways

Each time a student visits your office for a casual occasion, he or she should leave with two things – a smile and something with your hashtag. A student stops by with a cupcake for you on his birthday? He gets a high-five and a sticker with your hashtag. Two-inch round stickers can be ordered in great quantity and are perfect for these types of occasions. Magnets are also useful, especially the car magnets. Make one with your hashtag and they are the perfect giveaway for parents. You can put them on cars during Back to School Nights and also add some in the staff lot. Your staff will enjoy that recognition, too. Some will even keep the magnet for a while and then pass it along to someone else worthy of some recognition. Safety note – You will be tempted to take pictures of cars with your hashtag magnet while driving. Even while at a stop light, this is not safe. Don't let your temptations and excitement over the success of your program put you in a dangerous situation. You will understand the feeling we are talking about when you are stopped behind a car soon and see your hashtag!

Signage

Signs are so easy to order now from internet companies or local sign shops. The yard sign is a great way to promote your social media and they last a long time. Before your next school year, order a yard sign for each of your social media platforms (i.e. Twitter and Facebook), Remind text messaging (if you use it), your school's mission, and then, of course, a big welcome sign, too!

As we tell our school story on social media, we want to use traditional promotion devices to channel parents to our social media. #7StepStories

---

KEY TIPS – Reasonable Hashtag Swag

- T-shirts
- Car magnets
- Small round stickers
- Postcards
- Pencils, pens, or stylus
- Sunglasses
- Water bottles

Relationships

Education is a "people business" and relationships are most important. We need access to each other to form relationships. Twitter is likely the social media platform that gives the most direct access to individuals. When Twitter started becoming more commonly used, many users kept their profiles protected so that only their followers could see their tweets. However, as social media has become mainstreamed, users commonly hold a public profile. (Your school's account will need to be public to connect with the most people.)

Digital citizenship has come far enough that most in education are comfortable using a public profile as they know that they will use the account in appropriate ways. Twitter accounts are also verified, meaning that Twitter connects them to an email address, so they are a little more secure and also more likely to be used appropriately. Your school's Twitter account will be an effective vehicle for connecting with other organizations to share your school's story. Step 5 – Will Anyone Follow Me? – will explain using social media to increase your followers. Here, we are using social media to connect organizations to help spread an awareness that your school is on social media.

Twitter provides access that we have never had. It takes out the "middle man" and can connect you directly to local media and organizations in your area that can help to tell your school's story. So, use it to make connections with those in the media and also local organizations. Many media personalities maintain and run their own Twitter account. Connecting with them provides a chance for them to use your post on the evening news, their news station's website, or in a podcast. News personalities do this all the time and it is a quick way to reach your followers in different places. Many areas also have local newspapers, newsletters, or fliers and like to connect with schools. Having a go-to contact at each of these agencies is a must. Even if you only write a short article for them at the beginning of the year and the end of the year, it is still a traditional way to connect with people.

Think of all the things that happen at the beginning of the year. You can quickly list them and write an article easily as well. You have an open house, summer reading, fall athletics, new curriculum, a theme for the year, previews for special events, and many other things that you have planned for the summer and you want to share this excitement when students return to the halls. Write it all down, take a few pictures with students and your new hashtag t-shirts or holding some school pride merchandise, and send it to the newspaper. Yes, people still read them and students still love being featured in them!

Publicity and public relations can take you many other places where you can share your hashtag and make parents aware of your social media presence. Big events get big attention. Apply for your students to present at a conference and more people will follow your accounts. Look for poster sessions where students can meet with educational organizations and talk about your school. State school board associations often use these sessions to connect with students and schools at their own conferences.

Some organizations will allow you to make a promotional video for them as well. In 2015, the Garnet Valley Elementary School News Club created a promotional video for the Pennsylvania Educational Technology Expo and Conference (PETE&C). Students and the club sponsors spent a day at the conference in Hershey, Pennsylvania where they interviewed the keynote speaker, asked questions of organizers and participants, collected footage in sessions, and then edited and produced the video right there that day. As part of the experience, they wrote an article for the newspaper and shared their promotional video with their School Board. All of these events tell your story and now that you are building a social media presence, you will share these exceptional events in traditional media and direct the readers to see more on your social media pages.

Parent/Guardian Training

When the Common Core State Standards debuted, everyone made a huge attempt to explain the "new math." Schools held parents' nights, wrote and adopted new curriculum, sent home fliers, purchased a new textbook series, and created resources to aid parents in learning the new approach to math alongside their children. For many, social media is the same thing. It scares them, is misunderstood, or may feel forced. To build an excitement for telling our school's story on social media, we need to make parents comfortable. Part of this is in training and the other part is in helping students to be safe. For parents who use social media are more likely to talk with the children about safe and appropriate use, more likely to monitor them online, and more likely to have rules and limits for what is permitted.

To build an excitement for telling our school's story on social media, we need to make parents comfortable. #7StepStories

When we plan parent training, we need to think of parents as digital adopters. Many of them have learned to use technology but did not grow up with it. A digital native, like many of our students, would learn about social media through videos on YouTube or by going through Google search results. Many parents don't think like that yet. They wait to be taught because that is how they learned. So, instead of saying, "Go look it up," we need to be offering training from the ground up.

Parents of elementary school-age students are likely on Facebook. As their children get older, they usually migrate to Twitter to connect with their schools. Eventually, they will try to keep up with their children on Instagram and Snapchat, although these platforms are not yet used as often to tell your school's story. Rarely a parent needs some support with Facebook, but Twitter seems to be a lot more intimidating for parents. However, since it is easier to connect with other schools in your districts and systems on Twitter, it is likely that you will use it as your primary social media platform. So, we need to train parents to use Twitter more often than Facebook. Later, we will discuss how to connect different platforms so that posting is most efficient but for now let's get parents on Twitter.

Earning Twitter Wings

Twitter training can take place as part of another meeting, like a parent organization meeting, or can be a stand-alone offering. There is definitely plenty to learn but not so much that it should be intimidating. Once a parent creates a profile, you will have them connected to your schools in no time. Here are some recommended topics to cover in a Twitter training for beginners:

- What is Twitter? Common Sense Media has a brief, informative video posted on their site under the "For Parents" channel: commonsensemedia. org.
- Why use Twitter? To connect with your school and district, oversee student accounts, and for news or personal interests.

- Vocabulary. Cover the basics like tweet, retweet, like, mention, and hashtag.
- Sign up. Show parents how to sign up by creating a username, add profile and header pictures, and write a bio.
- Who to follow. Start by sharing Twitter handles for your school account and other accounts for your staff and district.
- Privacy settings. Talk with parents about their options for privacy.
- Tweet. Send a few tweets with the group, interact with others through likes, retweets, and replies.
- Hashtags. Share a list of parent-friendly hashtags like #PTchat, #edchat, #edtech, #education, and #elemchat.
- Direct messaging. A feature available on most social media platforms; be sure they know that students use this often.

After the overview of teaching new Twitter users, definitely leave time for practice and questions. After the meeting, consider sending a tweet welcoming your new users. When you see them interacting with your account in the future, make reference to the training that you did together when connecting with them online. This will encourage others to attend the trainings at school to get more comfortable with social media as well.

Digital Citizenship and Online Safety

In addition to your parent training, there are other resources that parents will find very helpful. Two excellent sites are Common Sense Media and NetSmartz. Common Sense Media (commonsensemedia.org) has sections for parents and for educators and covers topics from Family Guides to Marketing to Kids. NetSmartz (netsmartz.org) is a program of the National Center for Missing and Exploited Children (2017) that provides learning and training on multiple types of technology. NetSmartz has sites for kids, teens, parents, educators, and more. Training on social media can easily extend beyond your sessions with these resources.

Step 3 – Traditional Methods that Build a Social Media Following – connects parents to your school through the communication methods that you have used in the past along with new ideas to share your hashtag.

Reflecting on your current communication tools and their effectiveness will help you plan for using social media more. Your website and a consistent template for email will remind parents of your social media platforms. When you do see parents face-to-face you can use postcards, stickers, and magnets to send them home with something in their hands that reminds them of your school's social media presence. School spirit items are a fun way to keep spreading the word all year long. Everyone loves free stuff and your parent organizations can also help by designing spirit wear with your hashtag.

Relationships are key in building these bridges from the traditional to the contemporary. Feeding local media with news about how you are using social media and connecting directly with local news personalities will broaden the message in traditional locations. Relationships with local organizations will also gain more attention from parents as you share this news on your social media platforms. Finally, be sure to train parents on Twitter. They mostly know Facebook based on personal use. Teaching them how to use Twitter and providing additional resources so they can keep their children safe on social media will get them using social media more and create a larger audience for your school's story. Once you finish this checklist, everything in the plan from here on out occurs within your social media platforms:

Step 3 – School Leaders To Do List

1. Reflect on your current communications plan

2. Place links to your social media sites on your main website

3. Create a standard email template, like a digital letterhead, that includes links to all social media sites and your hashtag

4. Prepare for face-to-face meetings with parents by creating handouts, like postcards, that will direct them to your social media

5. Raise your school spirit with t-shirt design contests, unique hashtag t-shirts, free giveaways, and signage

6. Build relationships with local media and organizations to share what you are doing on social media

7. Train parents so that they are comfortable on Twitter.

Step 4 – Making It Happen

In Steps 1 through 3, you heard about tying your vision and mission into your social media presence as well as the use of hashtags to create your social media identity. You also learned about traditional ways to build a following. In this chapter, we will share how you can launch your social media platform. We will also discuss the importance of paying close attention to the policies that govern social media use in your district. This includes student privacy. Finally, we will share how to build an audience and meet your parents where they are on social media.

For the purpose of this book, we primarily use Twitter at both Clemens Crossing Elementary and Garnet Valley Elementary as the hub for our social media presence. This does not mean that you could not simply use Instagram or Facebook exclusively, or in addition to Twitter. Most of what we have discussed so far in this book can be applied to most social media sites.

 ## Know the Policies

No matter what your preference is for a social media platform for your school, it is best practice and extremely important to comply with and follow your school district's policy for social media use. Many school districts and jurisdictions throughout the country have updated their social media policies paving the way for school administrators and staff to use Twitter, Facebook, Instagram, or other common social media platforms.

Clemens Crossing Elementary (see Clemens Crossing Elementary School, n.d.) is part of the Howard County Public School System in Howard County, Maryland. The Howard County Public School System is governed by Policy 8080: Responsible Use of Technology and Social Media

(Howard County Public School System, 2016). That policy defines how we are permitted to use social media in schools.

> The Board of Education of Howard County is committed to providing equitable access to technology and social media to further the strategic goals of the Howard County Public School System (HCPSS). The Board believes that technology should be leveraged to improve instruction, business operations, and communications. The Board encourages the use of social media to enhance student and stakeholder engagement, facilitate collaborative communications, and increase global connections. The Board believes that as technology changes the ways that information is accessed, stored, communicated, and transferred, those changes provide new opportunities and responsibilities. The Board expects that all individuals will act in a responsible, civil, ethical, and appropriate manner when using technology for HCPSS-sanctioned activities.

Student Privacy Is Important

The policy statement focuses on the importance of social media to engage people while operating in a responsible, civil, and ethical manner. This is important when you are in charge of any school our school district. Additionally, part of being responsible is honoring parental preferences and wishes regarding student privacy.

In the Howard County Public School System and at Clemens Crossing Elementary School, our student management system and parent portal asks parents to choose if their child should be excluded from photographs and media coverage. This includes social media posts. Every month, at Clemens Crossing, we run a "Do Not Photo" report that generates a list of students who are on the "Do Not Photo" list. We keep that list available on our iPhones in the iBook app for quick reference. We do that so we can reference it while taking pictures to post on social media. The list helps us when we take pictures to make sure we honor the wishes of parents who choose to keep their children off social media, media coverage, or website postings. As a school and as a school district, it is very important to consider having a tool for parents to opt out of pictures and social media posts for their children at school.

Garnet Valley School District has an opt-out on its website and sends a notification to parents each year. Furthermore, we are very particular and careful with the privacy of our students. We work hard to make sure names are never associated with a picture of a student or student work. For example, when students held up their Spelling Bee certificate after the school-wide Spelling Bee, we asked the children to put down their certificates (which had their names printed on them) so we could take a picture to post on Twitter. When we walk around the school and visit classrooms, we make sure student names on desks or school work are not included in a picture on Twitter (see Garnet Valley Elementary School, n.d., Connect with GVE).

You can also use the markup in your photo app to redact student names. To use this, select a photo and then select edit. Click on the button for more tools and select markup. This tool will allow you to draw a line in many different colors through the student's name. We want to make sure people could not use a student's name to look up any identifiable information for ill-intended purposes. The use of Twitter is great to celebrate student success and achievement, but not at the expense of students' privacy and safety.

It is important to respect parental wishes regarding whether to include students in social media posts. #7StepStories

Garnet Valley School District policy refers to technology guidelines. The Social Media Guidelines (S. Mormando, email communication, May 20, 2015) for the district starts with:

> *The Garnet Valley School District recognizes the importance of using social media as a communication and learning tool. The purpose of these guidelines is to assist District employees, coaches, parents, and students in navigating the appropriate use of social media tools in their professional and personal lives. Social media includes any form of online publication where end users post or engage in conversation and include blogs, wikis, podcasts, virtual worlds and social networks.*

To this aim, the Garnet Valley School District has developed the following guideline to provide direction for instructional employees, coaches, students and the school district community when participating in online social media activities. The Garnet Valley School District social media guidelines encourage employees to participate in online social activities. But it is important to create an atmosphere of trust and individual accountability, keeping in mind that information produced by the Garnet Valley School District teachers and students is a reflection on the entire district and is subject to the district's Acceptable Use Policy.

KEY TIPS – Best Practices for Policies and Privacy

- Know your district's social media policy
- Do not include full names of children in your posts
- Provide parents with an avenue to opt out of social media posts
- Maintain a "Do Not Photo" list

School Twitter Accounts vs. Personal Twitter Accounts

Once local policy is in check, you are ready to establish a social media presence. On a related note, be aware how you want to represent your school. The Twitter app allows for you to have multiple Twitter accounts within one single Twitter app on all of your devices. You can toggle between multiple accounts. If you are on a computer, separate Twitter accounts or handles can be accessed with different usernames and passwords.

We believe it is very important to delineate between school, personal life, and professional life. We both have school Twitter accounts solely for use for school business. In addition, we have professional Twitter accounts for individual professional learning purposes (@PrincipalECos and @JMKotchEdD). We both use those accounts individually for professional collaboration and networking, professional learning, and educational Twitter chats to name a few.

Why would you have multiple accounts? We both believe it is important to separate your organization from your position within that organization. When you post for your school, you are posting on behalf of the school as an organization not you as a principal, teacher, or individual outside of work. Individually speaking, you might want to consider separating your professional world and personal world by having two personal Twitter accounts. Having a personal Twitter account separate from your professional account helps separate your personal life from your professional life. For example, you may want to keep religious and political philosophies out of your professional profile, but in your personal profile you can be more active. Using a personal account is recommended to begin learning a new social media platform.

You will definitely want to know how a platform works before trying it with your school's account. Having three accounts may sound like a lot but it is very manageable. You will appreciate having a school account separate from your professional and personal accounts. Remember, it is your school's story on Twitter and social media not your personal story.

It is very important to delineate between school, personal life, and professional life on social media. #7StepStories

---

KEY TIPS – Use Multiple Twitter Accounts

- School. This account is for everything about your school. Multiple people can use this account on behalf of the school.
- Professional. This account is for you in your professional capacity in whatever role you are in, and it can follow you and change as you change as a professional.
- Personal. This is where you can follow politics, religion, sports, and anything else you choose. Typically those topics should remain personal.

Setting Up Your Accounts and Pages

There are many resources available for those of you worried about setting up your accounts. You are deciding to set up a social media account on one of the major platforms, each of which has a very informative HELP section. YouTube also hosts instructional videos on setting up your accounts. Directions for setting up accounts can change often as the sites are updated. We provide some general guidelines as a way to show you that it's not hard! These directions below aren't intended to be followed step by step but will hopefully provide an overview so that you see that it isn't too involved. It's a good time to set up your account or accounts now.

Setting Up a Twitter Account for Your School

1. Go to www.twitter.com

2. Click the button for Sign up

3. Enter the name of your school

4. Enter your email (it will need to be an email not associated with another Twitter account)

5. Create a password

6. Enter your phone number and activate your account with the code sent to your phone

7. Choose a username that will be easy to search for and find

8. You can skip choosing your interests and also skip importing contacts

9. In the final step, search for and follow any other schools in your district

10. Skip the notifications for now

11. Take the tour and go!

12. Once familiar, add profile and background pictures and create your bio

13. Go through your setting and privacy information menus to select your desired levels

Setting Up a Facebook Page for Your School

1. You will need a personal Facebook account first so that you can add a page for your school to this account

2. Log in to your personal Facebook account

3. Click the down arrow at the top of the page and select Create Page

4. Click Company, Organization, or Institution

5. For the category, select Education or School

6. Enter the name of your school

7. Click Get Started

8. Add a picture and a cover

9. Create a Page @Username using your Twitter Handle

10. Add a short description including your hashtag

11. Go through Settings and set to desired security levels

12. Add any additional page administrators through Page Roles

Your two main accounts, if you choose to use both, are now set up. Your social media presence is starting to take shape and hopefully your excitement and inspiration is building. Check out some Twitter and Facebook accounts from other schools that you respect to get more ideas of what you can add to the setup of your pages. We will do some additional "technical" work below when we link the two sites. Now that you have these accounts, what are you going to do with them?

Your social media presence is starting to take shape and your excitement and inspiration is building. #7StepStories

 # Let's Get Posting

When the Howard County Board of Education revised its policy governing social media use in schools in July 2013, it paved the way to start using social media at Clemens Crossing Elementary and in each individual school within the district. We eagerly learned Twitter, and that paved the way to

share stories about our school with our community. If you are not sure what to do, start small. Follow other schools locally. Follow your school district. Retweet tweets that are relevant to your school.

When you are beginning your social media journey as a school, try to commit to share at least one tweet a day. Early on when we started to use Twitter, we did not know fully what to do. We made one goal for the year; to tweet at least once a day for the whole year. During that time, we published our Twitter handle on our website and in our newsletter. We met our goal of tweeting once a day, but that was mainly the extent of Twitter that year. It is okay to start slowly by tweeting once a day. Whether you start slowly with one or two tweets a day, or you go fast, it is important to be consistent. Building a following is important, but keeping that following engaged is even more important. Committing to frequent activity on your Twitter feed keeps your followers informed and interested in the content you want to share. If there are lengthy gaps of a few days, a week, or a month between tweets, you will lose your following. Your followers will not be engaged in the activity within your Twitter feed. The plan of at least one tweet a day worked and worked well for us. During the first year on Twitter, we had over 300 tweets at Bushy Park Elementary School, and that accumulated interest from a small following.

Building a following is important, but keeping that following engaged is even more important. #7StepStories

Accelerating Your Social Media Activity

The following year at Bushy Park Elementary, during the 2014–15 school year, we felt more comfortable with Twitter, and we were ready for the next steps. The next main goal was to build upon last year's following and expand our school's following on Twitter. We wanted to expand the topics and stories and share our school's story. We wanted to invest more time and energy into sharing our school's story. After attending a social media professional learning session at the NAESP (National Association of Elementary School Principals) Conference in Nashville in 2014, we learned about Storify.com as a tool to help build a following.

Storify is a social media website that provides users the ability to create timelines or stories using other social media sites such as Twitter, Facebook,

Instagram and even YouTube. Storify helped build a following by providing a platform to share Twitter activity without initially committing to joining Twitter. Using Twitter was pointless without a following. By using Storify initially, you can pull information from multiple social media sites and accounts to create a "Story" on Storify in one clean story line. We created a Storify profile (https://storify.com/bpes) for Bushy Park Elementary and then in 2015 at Clemens Crossing Elementary (https://storify.com/CCES_HCPSS). When we were trying to build a new following, we created Storify stories weekly. As the school year progressed, we changed the frequency of Storify stories to every other week or monthly. After the story was created on Storify, we used our email system to email all parents and community members on our email list serve. We did this for a few reasons.

Why Use Storify?

- Using Storify helped to build a following on Twitter.
- It included people who did not have Twitter.
- People who did not use Twitter were still able to see the same information and posts without formally being on social media.
- The only difference was the fact that people got Storify information periodically versus instantaneously on social media.

Using Storify illustrated to parents and community members that they could have a window on the world of what happens in our school. Sharing the information regardless of the access to social media seemed to have encouraged people to join Twitter or follow us on Facebook ultimately enhancing the engagement level. In addition to including everyone, it helped state the case for people to follow the school on Twitter. It was very clear that the use of Storify at both Bushy Park and Clemens Crossing Elementary Schools helped to increase our following on Twitter. Later in the book, we will share how you can monitor your social media effectiveness and gauge what people like to see on your Twitter feed. Using Storify helped to expand our following by more than double at Bushy Park Elementary and triple at Clemens Crossing Elementary. With a larger following, you have more people engaged in your story.

Linking Across Platforms

Another effective strategy we used to build a social media following for our school was to link Twitter to Facebook. Facebook too? You are probably saying, "No, I am not adding yet another thing on my plate!" The technology is there to link one or more social media platforms for cross-posting. After receiving feedback from a few parents about their preference for Facebook over Twitter, we learned there is a way to link Twitter to Facebook. This requires establishing or creating a Facebook page for your school.

After you create a Facebook page, you will need to go into the "Settings and Privacy" menu in Twitter. Click "Apps" and connect your Twitter account so it will automatically share your Tweets on your Facebook page. Most of what is posted on our Facebook accounts comes from Twitter. Two exceptions to this would be panoramic pictures and events. You can create an event on your Facebook page to generate interest in the event. You could also share this news through a tweet but creating the event on Facebook creates a page for the event and allows you to post more information like resources, ticket information, and links to generate interest.

Panoramic pictures can be taken in the Camera app on your phone. When panoramics are posted on Facebook, a mobile device user can move the phone around to see an expanded view of the photo and to have more interaction with it. Aside from events and panoramics, almost all of the activity on the Facebook page is generated automatically from Twitter. By linking Twitter to Facebook, we were able to customize our delivery of our social media message to engage people where they prefer to receive their social media information. The use of social media is then differentiated by platform to meet the need of the end user.

The use of social media is then differentiated by platform to meet the need of the end user. #7StepStories

Twitter and Facebook work well together in that you can post on Twitter and have your post look very similar when it automatically goes to Facebook. Instagram, however, is more of a stand-alone. There is no third-party app that can post on Instagram for you. That means that you can only post on Instagram from within the Instagram app itself. This prevents being able to post in one place and have it show up nicely on many platforms. You can post on Instagram and Instagram will send that post automatically to

Twitter; however, it will only show up as a link on Twitter. The user will not be able to see your text, photo, video, or any links. They will simply see a link on Twitter that they can click on to go to Instagram. If you follow this down the line, you would post on Instagram which would then send a link to post on Twitter which could send the same link to post on Facebook. Or you can post on Instagram, have Instagram send the post to Facebook (which works nicely) and have Facebook send the post to Twitter.

The challenge you run into is where you want to originate your posts. We prefer originating our posts from Twitter since Twitter is the most commonly used platform for connecting with other schools. The other schools in our district don't use Instagram as frequently so posts originating through Instagram would only be the content we created and we would lose all retweets from other district users of Twitter. Posting from Facebook to Twitter can also be a challenge as Facebook posts can be much longer than the 140 characters you can use on Twitter. So, posting automatically from Facebook to Twitter can truncate your post and not have it look as appealing for the users on Twitter. As you can see, there are many factors to consider. For these reasons, we use Twitter to post to Facebook and recommend posting separately on Instagram when you can for your Instagram users.

KEY TIPS – Be Innovative to Reach a Broad Audience

- Link Twitter to other social media platforms such as Facebook
- Use Storify.com to reach those who do not use social media
- Technology is always evolving, so continue to search for other ways to build and engage your audience

---

Your Devices Are Your Friends

Navigating the technology on your devices is also something where your confidence will grow with time. Below we provide you with a starter's guide to the apps and websites that we use on a regular basis. The list is divided by phone, tablet, and computer as screen size, accessibility, and memory requirements will vary for each application and purpose. Most of the apps and services are free. However, you will often find it better to upgrade to a paid version. Paid versions save you time by removing advertisements, provide more features, and create more user-friendly final products for your followers. Here is what we use:

Phone

> **Twitter:** the native app from the publishers of Twitter
>
> **Facebook:** the native app from the publishers of Facebook
>
> **Remind:** the native app from the publishers of Remind text messaging service
>
> **Collage apps:** Pic Collage, LiveCollage, Layout, Diptic, etc. – a variety of apps you can use to make collages when you want to join many pictures together into one post
>
> **Mematic:** an app for making memes with your own pictures and sayings or quotes
>
> **Flipagram:** a photo slideshow app where you can show many pictures one at a time
>
> **Vine:** an app that works with Twitter to record brief video clips, combine them into one, and share

Tablet

> **iMovie:** app version to create your own movies and also an easy way to add a title slide and credits to a slideshow of pictures and/or videos
>
> **Touchcast:** a recording system for recording videos for flipped or blended learning opportunities
>
> **Green Screen:** use your own pictures to create the background for your videos
>
> **Green Screen Animation:** make your own animations to put into your green screen videos
>
> **360:** a camera app that takes multiple photos and combines them into one 360 degree photo for an enhanced viewing experience

Quik: a super-fast slideshow app that offers many different themes along with music

Ripl: a slideshow app that combines photos quickly and easily

Superphoto: an app that lets you take a photo of someone you know and superimpose the faces into a new photo, background, or design

Chatterpix: take a photo, draw a mouth on it, make the mouth move, and a recording of dialogue

Cut & Paste: choose a photo, select part of the photo, add the part onto the background of another photo

Computer

Canva: an app that is easier to use on your computer to make your own digital content like an illustration to tweet about an upcoming event

Smore: a must for creating a weekly newsletter that is social media-friendly

YouTube: a site where you can create your own channel to upload video that is too long for Twitter

Google Drive: another place to upload longer video or to place files when you want to tweet a link to an attachment

Fotor: an internet-based photo collage site for the computer

Bit.do: a URL web shortener where you can customize the address and track your stats

Many of the apps and websites above can be used together in app-smashing. App-smashing is when you take several apps and utilize the special effects in all of them to make one final piece. For example, you can make videos through Green Screen and Chatterpix, combine them with a new photo from Cut & Paste, add all the media into iMovie, and end up with a video made by using several apps together.

Your topics to tweet are open and almost endless after establishing your accounts, beginning your social media presence, and considering the creative ideas above. The activity in a school building changes all of the time and your followers will be appreciative to know about it. Step 5 – Will Anyone Follow Me? – will provide more detailed information about the three categories of posts that we most commonly make: Informational, Celebratory, and Engagement posts. Ready to start before Step 5? Try a few of these quick ideas and jump in:

Informational

- Pictures of learning observed during instructional rounds or walk-throughs
- Give a heads up for an upcoming event
- Retweet something from your school district or another active user in the district

Celebratory

- Selfies with students coming off the bus
- Make a photo collage of students dressed up on a spirit day
- Group picture of students recognized for the weekly or monthly PBIS theme

Engagement

- Invite parents to a special event
- Post a Twitter poll
- Share a link to a video or to your website

Another way that we helped to make it happen was to encourage teachers to get involved in Twitter too. As a principal or an assistant principal, it is hard to see everything and be in multiple places at one time. If teachers and staff do not want to use Twitter, you can set up ways for teachers and staff to text or email you pictures and a brief description of a lesson, activity, accomplishment, or piece of news. Then you or the person in charge of social media can post the items on Twitter.

Teachers can also build a network or following on Twitter and share what goes on in their classroom, subject, and grade level. When teachers do that, then the school's Twitter account/handle can retweet and share the tweet from that teacher. As stated earlier in this chapter, it is also a good idea for teachers to separate their personal and professional lives if they choose to use Twitter. They should also consider what they want to post. If teachers want to post student work, they might want to use a social media platform and set higher security settings. They can have parents sign a release to share student work and then keep the account private to verify that only parents of the students in the class are viewing the content. You will be able to follow a private account after the teacher grants access but will not be able to retweet or share what they post. Teachers will need to have public accounts for you to share their posts. They can consider having a public account on Twitter for sharing and then use another platform like Instagram or SeeSaw to share student work in a more private setting.

Now that you have considered all of this information, you are ready to move forward and share your school's story. Make it happen!

Step 4 – School Leaders To Do List

1. Familiarize yourself with your district's technology and social media policies

2. Consider generating a "Do Not Photo" list for student privacy

3. Distinguish between personal and professional accounts as well as personal and organizational accounts when using Twitter

4. Go slow to move fast. Commit to tweet at least once a day

5. Build your following by cross-linking Twitter to Facebook

6. Use other sites such as Storify.com to share your story with people reluctant to use social media

7. Offer teachers and staff the opportunity to share with you or share on their own Twitter account.

Step 5 – Will Anyone Follow Me?

Step 5 asks a crucial question, "Will anyone follow me?" The answer to that question is contingent upon you as an administrator and the time and energy you put forth into this method of communicating with your community. This chapter contains ideas and suggestions based on our experiences using social media within our schools. We categorize the purpose or types of tweets to hook our followers into engaging bursts of information.

Engage Parents and Students

As a parent, imagine if you see something from your child's school on Twitter or Facebook that you can discuss at the dinner table. Parents could ask engaging questions periodically based on what they saw on their Twitter or Facebook feed. The conversation may sound like this, "It looks like you had an assembly today about your school's PBIS core values. What did you learn?" That discussion helps parents share with their children that they value education and what they do in school.

Imagine if you had the tool to learn about the topics covered in science, what the Next Generation Science Standards are, and how those standards are applied in school now. Imagine you could see an example of a teacher doing a Number Talk in the classroom. What is Hour of Code, and how did school incorporate coding in school? What is the Daily Five, and how do teachers use that as a structure during language arts? Parents can also follow hashtags for events like #ReadAcrossAmericaWeek, #GDD2017 (Global Day of Design), #GeniusHour, and more. The possibilities and topics are endless in a school setting. No matter what the topic is, these are some of the many examples of how administrators and teachers can tear down the walls of the school and share what's going on each day.

Information is powerful in so many ways, and providing that avenue for parents can only help to enhance a child's experience in school by strengthening the home to school connection. You cannot possibly do this without a plan to build your following or without a plan to engage your community through social media.

Becoming purposeful and deliberate with your social media plan, you can help create a stream of content useful for parents as they navigate an ever changing world of education. #7StepStories

Types of Posts

Part of making it happen is to make your content meaningful, relevant, timely and consistent. If you only occasionally share information on Twitter, you will not have anyone who will follow you. Becoming purposeful and deliberate with your social media plan, you can help create a stream of content useful for parents as they navigate an ever changing world of education. What topics do you choose to use and post? How do you know what is interesting to post? Where do you start? We generally categorize the content of our school's social media feed in three ways: **Informational**, **Celebratory**, and **Engagement**. We will explore some ideas for each of those three broad categories. Sometimes, those broad categories overlap, so we find that they are a good starting point when starting your social media journey.

Informational Posts about News and Events

Informing our parents and community about the day-to-day happenings at our schools is one of the primary uses of social media. Informational posts span a wide range of topics. From newsletters to PTA meeting reminders to evening activity notices to topics teachers teach in their classrooms, social media is a dynamic way to get your message out to your community. Incorporating information from the school's website is one way to get information out. Posting longer informational items on our school's website and tweeting the information helps to push out information. After information is posted on the website, you can copy and shorten the URL to paste it into a post or tweet.

Websites are great, and they provide a location for lengthy information. Unless you have an RSS feed (Rich Site Summary) where the site notifies you of updates, the information can often be lost. Copying the URL and sharing it with a short explanation pushes out the information you posted on your website. For example, when it is time to publish information about the science fair, you can post all of the information on the website. Once it is on the website, your social media post can be used to direct people to that information. That information may include a Google Form for the science fair registration and other resources people can use and download. All of the science fair information would be too much for a single tweet or post. By sending out the link, it gets the information out to the community. At the same time, it provides a location for people to refer to to access the information at a later date if needed.

Another example of informational tweets is the distribution of our bi-weekly newsletters, the Cougar Comments at Clemens Crossing and Weekly Announcements at Garnet Valley. We create the newsletters using the online program, Smore.com. Upon completion of the newsletter, the embedded URL shortener in Smore.com is copied and pasted in Twitter along with a short message stating that people can access the newsletter on our website or on Smore.com. Smore.com is easily recognized on Twitter, and it automatically creates a visually appealing preview on Twitter. Eventually, we send the link through our School Messenger and Schoolwires programs by email. Sending information by Twitter is easy, and you get your information out quicker than traditional email methods. Additionally, having our system for cross posting on Facebook, it automatically posts the newsletter on Facebook too. Information comes to us at a rapid rate. Having the ability to sift through that information and share it in a timely manner, can only benefit the people who seek to find their information in that format.

Informational Posts about Instruction

Twitter can also be used to inform parents about what is going on in your school and classrooms on a day-to-day basis. While walking through the school and classrooms, it is very easy to snap a picture on your phone and write 140 characters. Recently, in a first grade classroom during math, students were in the middle of a lesson about telling and writing time in hours and half-hours using analog and digital clocks. A few pictures were taken and uploaded on Twitter along with a quick sentence, "Don't be late! First graders are learning how to tell time."

You can even go deeper with specific strategies. One major initiative in math at CCES is the use of Number Talks to build number sense in kindergarten through fifth grade. You can easily "teach" parents what a Number Talk is by taking a few pictures and briefly explaining the number sense strategy. It is great to be able to snap a picture or take a video of students engaged in a science investigation. Sharing their thoughts and expressions through social media is a way to inform parents of moments in the classroom and school they otherwise would never see.

The use of Twitter allows for schools to follow reputable educational Twitter handles such as Education Week, Scholastic, or NEA. Retweeting reputable curricular and content-specific information on Twitter can help share information as well. Education changes all of the time. This type of information sharing is an easy platform to use to share current-day methods of teaching. There is no shortage of informational topics to share on Twitter in any school. There are plenty of standards to cover and share over the course of a year in every school. Teachers have unique and individualized ways they implement lessons.

Informational Posts about Safety

At the beginning of the school year, it is important to share day-to-day routines for students and parents to learn and follow. This helps to establish a safe routine from day one. For example, we publish directions, arrival, and dismissal procedures along with an aerial map of our school. In addition to sending that information by email, we post it on our website and tweet the graphic and directions on Twitter. Throughout the school year, informing parents about the school's emergency plan, emergency drills, and fire drills helps to affirm the importance of emergency planning as part of the school's plan. Whenever there are fire drills or emergency drills, we share that those drills occurred. Additionally, we share the purpose of the drill and when it would be used. Pictures can be shared of drills and links can be sent out by Twitter as well to share more detailed information. Furthermore, child-friendly resources can be shared with parents about how to talk to your child about emergencies at school and at home and how to respond to those potential situations.

Informational Posts about the School and Surrounding Community

Recently, there was #BikeToSchoolDay. This encouraged students to ride their bikes to school. It provides an opportunity to educate and inform families about the health benefits of biking, safe biking practices, and the reduction of carbon emissions by biking. In Columbia, Maryland, there are over 90 miles of bikes paths in the planned community. We even added information from the Columbia Association, the local parks and recreation association, about their biking app to help navigate through the 90 miles of pathways in the community. You do not need to capture everything. Sharing information over time gives parents and stakeholders a glimpse into what schools look like these days. Furthermore, by providing family-friendly information about the community and activities, we are able to build a positive, vibrant, and active community.

The content you share does not only have to be related to curriculum and instruction. There are hundreds of activities and events each year in schools. At the middle school and high school levels, there are athletics programs and teams, school clubs, and the arts. Schools have a wide variety of programs and events both during and after school. Sharing upcoming reminders for any event or activity through Twitter is a natural way to engage families and pull them into the school after hours. Furthermore, being able to retweet important community reminders such as Board of Education meetings or registration for summer camps through the parks and recreations programs helps inform and engage families and communities outside of school. All of these events and activities provide endless topics and possibilities for administrators as they share what goes on in their schools.

KEY TIPS – Informational Posts

- Plan what you are going to post at the beginning of each week by looking at upcoming events on your calendar
- Monitor your school's Twitter feed and retweet important informational items
- Tweet information from your school's newsletter in small chunks

Celebratory Posts: Recognizing Success and Achievements

Celebrating achievement and accomplishments opens up even more great topics to tweet and post. Celebrating and recognizing people is a great way to reinforce best practices. Schools can recognize students, teachers, staff members, parents, and volunteers. The possibilities are wide open in this category as well. Recognizing people on social media provides an avenue to focus on positive achievements and great things going on in your school, schools throughout your district, and even schools all over the country. Who does not like some sort of recognition? Two examples follow:

Systems of Support

As a PBIS (Positive Behaviors Interventions and Supports) school, Clemens Crossing Elementary School recognizes one student from each classroom every Friday. Each child gets a positive phone call home. In addition, students get to be part of a group picture. That picture is added to a bulletin board, and the group picture is posted on Twitter. Garnet Valley Elementary posts pictures from its #jaguarmax program to let parents know who was recognized and also what the new theme is for the upcoming month. Parents frequently comment and interact with those posts on Twitter and Facebook. It is great to see the level of excitement that one tweet can generate. When a parent posts a question it helps us to know what needs to be better explained. We learned we needed to inform parents what PBIS is when they commented, "What is PBIS?" in a reply after a post. This gave us an opportunity to tweet about PBIS and how we celebrate and recognize positive behaviors.

Community Engagement

Each year, the Howard County Public Library encourages elementary school children to engage in the Rube Goldberg Challenge where they have to design a machine or system to solve a problem. Students design, create, test, and run their system. Once they become successful with the challenge, they video record their group's system or machine. It is submitted and posted to the Library's YouTube account for a panel to judge. The culminating event is an awards celebration. This is a great way to promote the school and celebrate students. Posting pictures of the students and their accomplishments helps create an environment where students can take risks to learn in a safe environment. We were even able to share their YouTube video of their #RubeGoldberg challenge machine on Twitter. This builds interest and excitement by celebrating students' accomplishments while encouraging future engineers to take on the challenge.

Another example of recognition overlaps with how we inform people about curriculum and lessons taught in a particular class. Think about the teacher who taught the lesson about time as described in the previous section. How do you think that teacher must have felt when she was part of a lesson that was posted on Twitter? As long as you tell your staff ahead of time how you use Twitter and to notify you if they prefer not to be recognized that way then you can tweet naturally throughout the day. If they do not mind, then being recognized that way sure must help the teacher feel celebrated and accomplished when their lesson was posted on Twitter. Celebrating accomplishments such as winning the Spelling Bee or racing in the 5K fundraiser race helps to reinforce a culture of learning, perseverance, and taking risks. If you are always on the look-out for students, staff, and teacher accomplishments, you can be on your way to having a culture of openness within your school.

Celebrating and recognizing people is a great way to reinforce best practices. #7StepStories

---

KEY TIPS – Celebratory Posts

- Look for ways to celebrate
- Recognizing students and teachers will help reinforce great learning and work habits

---

Engaging Posts

Engagement is important in every school. How can you use social media to engage stakeholders? Social media is a dynamic tool to use to be able to solicit feedback and input. Twitter chats are a popular way to solicit input and feedback from your community. On the high school level, you could engage in a Twitter chat with students to get their ideas and feedback as well. Parents, teachers, and administrators have busy lives. It is hard to balance school life and the many different places you need to be in your personal life.

Engage Through Twitter Chats

One way Twitter is unique is through the ability to connect. Participating in Twitter chats using a professional Twitter handle gives you opportunities to learn and connect with people in your school community or around the world. For this example, Clemens Crossing wanted to try to engage families using a Twitter chat. Twitter chats are public conversations where individual tweets are linked together through a unique hashtag. The hashtag allows you to follow and participate in the discussion.

Many schools conduct listening forums such as a coffee and conversation with school administration. Clemens Crossing Elementary School looked at a school Twitter chat as an opportunity to have that type of conversation without having to leave your house. Two Twitter chats were conducted early in a school year. One was a Back to School chat and the other was a chat that focused on the topic of building culture. The chats were pre-scheduled. They included a publication about the format of Twitter chats (Q1, A1 format of questions and answers and the importance of including the unique hashtag in each question and answer). Although only a dozen people participated the first time, we were able to get valuable information and feedback from the community. As you learned in the previous chapter when we talked about Storify.com, you can pull all of the questions and responses and make a Storify.com "story" and publish that after the chat. This way, people can review the public conversation.

Direct Feedback

Twitter and Facebook give schools opportunities to gather feedback directly. If you pose a question, you can generate feedback in the form of a poll on Twitter. For example, you can post a tweet, "Are you going to come to International Night tonight?" In the same tweet, give the end user the opportunity to interact with the tweet by giving them the choices, "Yes, No, or Next year." If you want to solicit more feedback, you can create a survey on Google Drive or SurveyMonkey and post the link to your Twitter feed. Another method of engagement is simply asking for people to interact with Twitter or Facebook posts. People can write ideas, statements, or questions on posts. You can also encourage people to send direct messages to those accounts if they feel they want to interact that way. This type of engagement through Twitter allows for schools to send out reminders and gauge interest for an activity or program and also solicit feedback for continuous improvement.

KEY TIPS – Engaging Posts

- Use Twitter chats to promote ideas, feedback and discussion
- Use Twitter polls for a quick-click feedback
- Use the reply feature on Twitter or comments on Facebook to provide a place for people to ask questions or provide input

---

Social media is a dynamic tool to use to be able to solicit feedback and input. #7StepStories

Getting Seen and Noticed

Most social media platforms used to operate in chronological order. As platforms try to provide a better user experience and also increase revenue through advertisements, some have changed the order in which posts appear in your feed or timeline. Twitter can still operate mostly in chronological order if you unclick the "show best tweets first" setting; however, it will mix in tweets that you have missed and might want to see. It also won't load your entire timeline on your mobile device if you weren't recently in the app. Facebook and Instagram now show you what they think you would want to see first using an algorithm. This makes it hard to be sure that all of your posts will be noticed by your followers.

Alerts and Tweet Notifications

There are a few ways to increase the likelihood that your followers see your posts. The first way is to educate your followers on how to set their notifications. Notifications vary depending on the platform but the overall idea is consistent. You need to get your followers to set their notifications so that they get an alert when you post. If you post at reasonable times and only post valuable information then your followers won't get annoyed with the alerts. Your followers can select the type of alert that they prefer. They can choose in-app alerts which mean that when they go into the app they can find a list of notifications about what people they follow have posted. These alerts are called notifications in Twitter, Facebook, and Instagram. They can also get alerts on their phone which will appear whether or not they are in the app or they can get an email sent to them when you post.

As Twitter users ourselves, we set our own alerts and notifications. We have notifications set in the apps for posts from people we don't want to miss and have additional alerts on our phones should a tweet come from our district or the superintendent. Facebook has an additional feature where you can set new posts from certain users to appear first in your timeline. If your followers are on Facebook, you will want them to go to your page so that they can Like your page and also Follow your page. Once they Follow your page, they can set the priority order for your posts by clicking on the arrow next to "Following" on your Facebook page. You will want them to set your posts to appear first so that they see the school's posts as soon as they go on their newsfeed. You can also go through your Facebook notifications after a post and see who Likes your post. You can then invite anyone who Likes your post to also Like your page. This will show your posts in the newsfeed without needing another one of their friends to Like a post so that they see it too.

Overcoming Privacy Settings

Some parents and guardians will not Like or Follow you on social media because they don't understand privacy settings. By following you on Facebook, Twitter, or Instagram, parents are not giving up any of their privacy. You still will only be able to see what they have posted publicly if they have a private account. In other words, following an account doesn't automatically give that account access to your private information, postings, or friend/follower lists. Parents who want to keep their social media private can do so by setting their accounts to private. As the user of the school's social media accounts, we don't request to follow any parents. We only follow professional accounts along with schools and organizations within schools. Even if we did request to follow parent accounts, the parents could decide whether or not to accept that request and therefore allow us to see their posts. However, we have no interest in mixing our professional and organization platforms with parents' personal social media. Facebook "friends" confuse some people because when you are friends on Facebook you share your photos, videos, friend lists, and more. This is not true of "Following" an account. "Following" an account only puts the posts from that account into your feed or timeline. It does not give any access to the parents' posts or information.

Moderating Comments and Monitoring Followers

The accounts and pages that we set up for our schools are public and available to anyone on social media. We set them up this way so that we don't need to approve every follower because it would be impossible to verify if each follower were really connected to our school. We often have followers who are relatives – grandparents, aunts, uncles, cousins, etc. – of the students in our school. We wouldn't even be able to match the last names with the students in our schools. We also know that we are going to post appropriately and safely. We do our best not to post student faces and names together and we only post material that is in line with our school policies, practices, and procedures. Unfortunately, we can't always guarantee the same level of respect from our followers and others who interact with our platforms. For this reason, we have some decisions to make about how often we are going to monitor our social media.

If you are going to check your social media often for inappropriate comments or for followers whose social media presence doesn't match your purposes, you might want to stick to one platform so that you can manage moderating your presence. If you understand that you are posting appropriately and that people will not cast a shadow on you if someone else interacts inappropriately with your social media, then you are probably okay to have more than one platform. You will also be able to rely on your other followers who will be likely to report inappropriate comments through flagging them on each platform or notifying you.

To monitor comments on your platforms, it is best to turn on your notifications for comments. You can also set notifications for other interactions. If you get a notification for an inappropriate comment, you can quickly delete the comment on your Facebook post or remove the tweet on your

Twitter page. You will also want to scroll through your followers from time to time. The more followers you get and interactions you have, the more likely it will be that businesses and online "trolls" will follow your accounts to try to get your followers to look at their pages. When scrolling through your followers list, you can block anyone who is not following you for your intended purposes. It is good to get into a habit of monitoring your accounts and pages. It's also exciting to see how much interaction you are getting. We will look into the analytics more in Step 6 – Is It Working? For now, just know that you can check your notifications on both Twitter and Facebook in a matter of minutes each day once you have your notifications set up for the content you want to be alerted to.

Breaking News and Sneak Previews

The final piece of earning more followers is showing them the benefits of social media. Many people are getting the majority of their information from social media now. If you want to move your school's community away from traditional methods like your website and emails then you will need an incentive for them to get their information from your social media. The incentive is in giving them information first on social media. In many ways this is so easy. If your only usual communication is a weekly newsletter then social media users will quickly see that they can learn a lot more about what goes on in school on a regular basis by seeing multiple posts most days. You can also release your newsletters on social media the night before you send an email with the information. If you live in an area where school closings occur due to inclement weather then you can post or retweet the school closing information through social media before beginning the usual processes of automated phone calls, emails, and website postings. Any opportunity to gain a new follower is a good one. That's why we tie together traditional marketing like in Step 3 with strategies to use online.

Schools have a great opportunity to take control of the message and share the endless positive stories in schools throughout the country. #7StepStories

Overall, we live in a time where information is shared at a fast rate and the expectation is for information to be available spontaneously and instantly.

Whether you turn on the news or scroll through social media feeds, a significant portion of news and information can be negative. We often hear what's wrong with society followed by everyone's opinion about what's wrong if you go through the comments. Schools have a great opportunity to take control of the message and share the endless positive stories in schools throughout the country. Schools can highlight accomplishments and achievements of students as well as success stories about teachers and classes. The opportunity to share this information in a positive manner can change the narrative in schools to "what's strong" not "what's wrong" with our schools and education. Hopefully, this communication will lead more people into believing that education is a solution to the troubles of society. Step 6 – Is It Working? is next once you complete the assignments below.

Step 5 – School Leaders To Do List

1. Make a plan to schedule sharing of informational items in a routine and consistent manner

2. Circulate throughout your school and look for celebratory items to share

3. Think about ways to engage families and pull them into the conversation about your school

4. Educate social media users on notifications, privacy, and priority settings

5. Examine your comfort level with moderating your sites

6. Show some love to your social media users with advance previews.

Step 6 – Is It Working?

You have been using Twitter to tell your school's story for a while now. You tweet and retweet a lot of content, share posts and stories, and you feel it is important as you share your message. Once information is posted, it is interesting to review the data periodically to determine what people pay particular attention to on your social media feeds.

By the Numbers

Twitter Analytics is a great place to start if you are looking for data to inform your social media strategy. Twitter Analytics is a powerful tool to help you monitor your effectiveness on their social media platform. Twitter Analytics is also a free tool embedded into your Twitter account once you initially log in to the analytics site. In order to access Twitter Analytics, you have to do a one-time set-up by going to analytics.twitter.com. It will ask you to log in to your Twitter account. By doing this, you are ready to reflect upon your Twitter activity. Twitter Analytics is located in the profile pull-down menu under your picture. Exploring Twitter Analytics gives you a wealth of information about the type of content people interact with the most.

Once you are in the Twitter Analytics section, the Account Home will give you a summary of your account history and trends for the past 28 days. You'll notice that all of these data graphics are fairly intuitive and do not require any training or an advanced degree in statistics to decipher or interpret. All that is required is knowing what to look for and knowing how to use this information to make any necessary changes in your posting habits. The analytics features will give you raw data regarding the number of tweets, tweet impressions, profile visits, mentions, and new followers.

Once a month has concluded, it will give you that information in a historical perspective of each month. We always find it interesting to see which tweet was the most impressionable each month. How can you figure out what people are paying particular attention to within your Twitter feed? How do you analyze and use your Twitter data? There are many questions you can ask when reflecting upon your Twitter activity. Ask yourself some of these guiding questions to gauge your effectiveness and efficiency on Twitter.

What Do People Want to See?

- What do people pay particular attention to in your social media stream?
- What types of tweets receive the most engagement? What are the characteristics of the tweets? Do they include images? Videos? Links to articles?
- Did long or short tweets receive more engagement? Should I tweet more within that character count?

Who is your audience?

- Who are you reaching?
- How many people are following you?

When is a good time to tweet?

- What time of the day did my tweets get the highest engagement? Should I schedule a tweet every day around that time?
- Should I tweet more about the topics that got more attention?

What about future tweeting?

- How can I incorporate those popular elements into future tweets?
- How does my recent Twitter engagement performance compare with the previous month? What factors changed the performance for the particular period? What change prompted the increase or decline in engagement on Twitter?

Who's Following Us on Social Media?

You can learn everything from how your following has grown over time all the way to conversation tracking on your Twitter feed. Many social media platforms have tools to help you analyze. In addition to Twitter Analytics, Facebook pages have a similar tool to help you measure and analyze your activity, called Insights. In the corporate world, these are tools to help companies market their products or services. In the education field, you can use portions of the Analytics and Insights tools too. Paying to boost or promote your information to a larger audience would only be recommended for specific purposes. If you build your following, you can reach your intended audience without paying for advertisements. Although you are not selling or advertising anything, you can use the tools to see what your community is focused on when you are telling your school's story. By becoming well informed and reflective with your Twitter Analytics, you will help yourself learn what catches people's eye and interest. While looking at the data, knowing what questions to ask about your data will help you improve your Twitter content strategy.

KEY TIPS – Set up tools to monitor your social media activity

- Activate Twitter Analytics
- Use Facebook Pages Insights

By becoming well informed and reflective with your Twitter Analytics, you will help yourself learn what catches people's eye and interest. #7StepStories

In Step 5, we discussed building a following. Monitoring data while you are building a following is important. In a way, part of building your following is related to analyzing your tweeting habits. We stated earlier that building a following can be a challenge, so you have to make sure you are posting meaningful information. Meaningful and interesting social media posts draw people into your Twitter feed and into your Twitter account.

In addition to engaging content, consistency is key. You want people to expect regular daily information. Luckily, schools are a perfect place to share new information daily. Both at Garnet Valley Elementary and at Clemens Crossing Elementary Schools, we use Twitter as the primary social media platform that is also connected to Facebook. Posting information daily is part of how we operate in this social media age.

Who Is Your Audience?

In a school setting, who are you focused on reaching? In an elementary school, your primary audience are your parents, teachers, and staff. You might promote Twitter to keep your broader community informed. You may also use Twitter to help your colleagues in your district's central offices stay informed. At our schools, our main goal is to help inform parents about the day-to-day excitement and inspiration in our schools. The Analytics feature within Twitter will help you answer this series of questions.

- How many people are following you?
- Who are you reaching?
- Are people paying attention?

Let Data Guide Your Social Media Plan

We want to focus on building our audience and keeping the audience after we get followers. One of the features on the main page of your Twitter profile is the number of followers you have at any given time. You can see that without active analytics embedded into your Twitter settings. The Twitter Analytics allows you to monitor Twitter followers over time. You can see a record of trends for your following each month to help you figure out why there were increases (or decreases).

Frequent Tweeting Is Essential

People tend to join and follow Twitter when there is frequent and interesting information to interact with in the Twitter feed. In order to build and maintain interest, we increased the frequency of tweets. At Clemens Crossing and Garnet Valley, we both currently have a general goal of tweeting one to five tweets per day. As stated before, the tweets focused on information, celebrations, and ways to engage people. We focus on what students were working on in school, products students made in school, and disseminating information to our community.

Engaging the Reluctant Follower

Tweeting is easy to do, but as we discussed in Chapter 4, once we accumulated a series of meaningful and interesting tweets, we used Storify.com to build followings. Storify is a social media platform that allows the user to pull posts and tweets from a variety of sites into one "story." At Clemens Crossing, we pulled a series of tweets from our @hcpss_cces Twitter feed and made a story from the previous two to four weeks. Then the Storify link was sent to our community using our internal email list. You can visit the Storify pages at the website, storify.com/CCES_hcpss. This was a very effective strategy at the beginning of the 2015–16 school year. We increased the number of Twitter followers at Clemens Crossing Elementary from 250 to 375 by the second week in September 2015. By December of that year we had 475 followers. Storify was the tool we used to hook people into the same information from Twitter without initially having to set up an account. The people who were (and may always be) reluctant to follow on Twitter were able to see the same information.

KEY TIPS – Monitor Analytics

- How often are you tweeting? Monitor tweets over time
- Look at your engagement rate periodically
- Are you growing your following? Check out growth over time
- Get to know your followers/audience. Who is following you and from where?

Making Social Media Part of Your School's Culture

Now that we had a regular stream of tweets, we continued to publicize our Twitter account. We asked people to follow our Twitter page during Back to

School nights, in welcome letters, on our website, and in communications home. Monitoring the number of followers and views was important to determine how many people we reached. We found that as our Twitter following increased the number of Storify views decreased. We continued to use Storify in order to continue to engage people who did not want to subscribe to Twitter or Facebook.

Data helped inform us on the frequency with which we used Storify. After a few years of using this strategy, it was more useful at the beginning of the school year to help hook new people into Twitter or Facebook. The Twitter and Facebook followers for Garnet Valley Elementary School have grown consistently each year also through tools like Storify and traditional methods. The Facebook and Twitter followers have increased by around 200 additional followers for each platform each year since Twitter began being used in 2013 and Facebook in 2015.

Looking Closely at Who Follows You

The Audiences tab is another section located in the menu bar within the Analytics. That tab provides basic information about the people who follow you. The only relevant information, in our opinion, is under the demographics button. For example, when you look at the Audiences tab for Clemens Crossing Elementary, you would see that the school has a 68% female and 32% male following. According to snapshot data, 28% of our followers are between the ages of 25 and 34. The age range of 35 to 44 years old is similar, making up 27% of our followers. This information helps to illustrate that mothers with school-aged children are the primary audience for the @hcpss_cces Twitter account. Yes, that makes sense! Do we really need this information? Maybe. Some of the information is useful for businesses, but age and gender data in the demographics page makes sense for an elementary school. We can also tell that 98% of our audience is from the United States. The percentage of our audience from Maryland is 78%. This means that 22% of our audience is from outside of our community. Those followers could be relatives or businesses who are related to education. If a majority of our followers were not from Maryland, or they were all over 55 years of age, then we would not be reaching our community or the age range of parents who typically have elementary aged kids. Looking closely at who is following you will help you determine if you are reaching your intended audience. If you are, good! If your data looks off considerably, you may want to figure out a new strategy to reach your intended audience.

What Do People Want to See?

Building a following is one thing, but keeping the momentum going is the hard part. At our two schools, Twitter is used to purposefully push out important information. Newsletters and website information are pushed through Twitter and Facebook in addition to sending the information out by email. Newsletters are posted on the websites, and URL shorteners are used to post the URL in a tweet, so the newsletter can be tweeted out. At Clemens Crossing, the communication plan can be considered "purposefully redundant." Information is disseminated multiple times in a variety of ways. This allows for parents to choose their preferred method to receive that information. The school website is full of up-to-date information that changes periodically. In order to notify people of the changes, updates and links to longer pieces of information are shared through Twitter. With all that information flowing on a regular basis, it is important to figure out what people pay attention to.

Tweaking Tweets

The Twitter Activity page highlights a wealth of information about each individual tweet you send out. By looking at the tweets section of the analytics page, you can monitor tweet activity, top tweets activity, and much more. Initially, you can see the engagement rate percentage for each tweet you post. According to Twitter (support.twitter.com/articles/20171990), "impressions" are the number of times a tweet was sent to a user's feed. "Engagements" means the total number of times a user has interacted with a tweet. That includes all clicks anywhere on the tweet (including hashtags, links, avatars, or username). The engagement rate is calculated by dividing the number of engagements by the number of impressions. Periodically, we look at those three pieces of data to help get feedback about our Twitter activity.

The next tab is the Tweets tab. This allows you to dig deeper into your Twitter activity and engagement rates. Immediately, you will find two interactive bar graphs. Each bar represents one of the past twenty-eight days. The lower bar graph tells you the number of tweets for that particular day. The bar graph above that shows the number of account impressions for that day. Located below the interactive bar graphs are summaries of each tweet for that time period. You can find out the number of impressions, or the number of times a Twitter user saw that particular tweet. You can also find the engagements for each tweet. That is the number of times someone interacted with the tweet. Then, Twitter Analytics calculated the engagement rate (engagement rate divided by impressions). Why do you want to know this information? The greater the engagement rates, the greater the interest for particular information. You can use the interactive information to help you understand what people focused on so you know what to post in the future. You can go back and forth between the Tweets tab that shows analytical information in chronological order or you can click on the tab, Top Tweets. Top Tweets lists your tweets with the greatest engagement rates. It is good to be able to review that information and filter that data to help you understand what people are interested in seeing.

Similar to Twitter Analytics, Facebook Insights is a tab within a Facebook page. You can customize the viewed information by day, week, or month. Within a certain time frame, you can view the number of times people viewed your page and whether or not they liked the page. You can also see how many people liked or followed you on Facebook. Most importantly, just like Twitter, you can look at each post and see how many people you reached each time you posted on Facebook.

As we look back at one day over the past month, we see we had four tweets on a particular day with 4,500 impressions that day. Yes! That means that tweet could have been seen up to 4,500 times! Yes, you have a powerful tool to share your school's story when you can get that many impressions from one tweet. This ultimately helps you customize what your followers are more drawn to see. Interestingly, the analytical data for Garnet Valley Elementary is very similar for Twitter and Facebook. Twitter posts have created around 6,000 impressions a week while the Facebook post reach for GVES is also around 6,000 people per week. Clemens Crossing has very similar statistics for both Twitter and Facebook as well. The range for Twitter impressions is in the range of 5,000 to 7,000 per week. Facebook reaches are growing as more and more discover and like the page. They typically reach 2,000 to 4,000 a week on Facebook.

As we analyze and look at individual tweets and posts over a period of time, it is no surprise that social media posts that receive the greatest interest, attention, impressions, or reaches are those that highlight people. The analytics and insights tools help reaffirm that one way to engage your community is to highlight the children and people in the school. It is great to use that free tool to celebrate the accomplishments of your students, staff, and people that make your school a vibrant community.

The top post on Facebook at Garnet Valley Elementary during the 2016–17 school year involved connecting with a local news station. A few students got together and tweeted a question during a heat wave to a television morning show's meteorologist. The students wanted to know if a heat wave was going to break the record high temperature for the day. The meteorologist, her co-anchors, and others from the station retweeted their question and also played it on the morning news show the next day. The tweet was automatically sent to the school's Facebook page as well. During the week of this tweet and post, the total page views increased by 286%, over 6,000 people were reached, and the post engagements went up by 212%! The video of the newscast went to 2,000 in the first day!

Deeper analytics also show when your followers react and interact with your posts. #7StepStories

In addition to analyzing past data, we also survey our parents to plan for future posts and initiatives. The surveys we have conducted have been to understand the communication preferences of our families. You can consider the following questions for communication surveys:

- On a scale of 1–5, how well does the communication from our school inform you of upcoming and important events?
- How do you prefer to receive exciting news from our school? Website, email, text message, social media, phone call, other.
- What social media platforms do you use? Twitter, Facebook, Instagram, other.
- How comfortable are you following our social media accounts? Very comfortable, somewhat comfortable, uncomfortable, not sure.

- Would you attend future training on social media if provided by the school? Yes, no, maybe.

- How often do you check social media? Once an hour or more, about twice per day, daily, weekly or more, never.

- What suggestions do you have for enhancing our school's communication plan?

Twitter Analytics and Facebook Insights provide enlightening information about what your followers want to see, who your followers are, when they check social media, and what types of posts they like to see. Deeper analytics also show when your followers react and interact with your posts. All of this helps in preparing for future tweets. While tweets that include many students have the highest probability of reaching the largest audience due to the number of students in the post, inspiring and remarkable events tend to have the highest engagements. Being able to highlight student achievements and accomplishments provides the canvas for creating a positive image of schools all over the world. This movement starts small with each school and then grows. First, schools connect within the districts. Then districts connect within the state as states connect within our country. Our 7 Steps are the story of how we started the momentum in our schools. It is our hope that sharing this plan through our book expands our connections to others in education as you build your own momentum and share your stories. We look forward to hearing them! You are on the right track to successfully share your school's story. You can work on the task list below and pause here for now while you increase your social media presence or you can jump into some new ideas to expand what you do in Step 7 – What's Next?

Step 6 – School Leaders To Do List

1. Link your Twitter account to Twitter Analytics

2. Find your Insights on Facebook

3. Monitor your Twitter feed

4. Examine your audience, timing of posts, and statistics for impressions, engagement, and post reach

5. Gauge what people like to see and create future posts that match interests

6. Celebrate your top posts

7. Inspire another school leader to share their school's story on social media.

Step 7 – What's Next?

We are on a continuous journey in education of innovating and improving. This journey has no station or destination at the end. We hope that the first six steps in this book have significantly moved you along in your journey of sharing all of the amazing things going on in your school. It is incredibly important for us to be advocates for public education. We need to fill the news about education with stories of the good things occurring every day. Our ultimate goal remains in seeing the success of our students as their achievement in PreK-12 education prepares them to contribute to our society and economy everywhere from our local communities to the international world. We need the support of our stakeholders who will ultimately hold the votes that will choose our legislators. Hopefully, these elected officials will choose to support our schools.

As principals, we share our stories as we also support our state and national associations who advocate for the children in our schools. Seeing photos and videos of our stories in places like Twitter and Facebook connects the accomplishments of our schools with the rest of the world. Let's share our stories as we connect digitally with others.

Let's share our stories as we connect digitally with others. #7StepStories

This chapter is different from the other chapters in that it is simply a list of ideas we've collected through our daily interactions with other connected educators like Tom Martellone (@TomMartellone), Michael Donnelly (@Dr_Donnelly_WD), and Keith Kuwik (@KeithKuwik). You might be ready for this chapter now or you might come back to it later. It's designed this way so you can quickly reference different ideas to tell your story using new tools whenever you are ready for more or something new.

We also hope to continue this chapter through sharing on our own social media platforms.

You can connect with us on Twitter (7StepStorytellers or @7StepStories) and Facebook (7 Steps to Sharing Your School's Story or @7StepStories) to add your own ideas to this list using #7StepStories. Staying connected keeps us fresh with continual ideas. Connect with us online and continue the conversation about Step 7 – What's Next? This chapter will include tools of the trade, enhancing photos and video, increasing interaction and engagement, and tips and tricks. Have fun with the ideas!

Tools of the Trade

Drones

Drones have been in the news as they are now often used by the military and are also starting to be used for commercial deliveries of small packages. They are being used to deliver medicine in remote areas, as well. The most common drone use is in photography as drones can get images at a reasonable cost compared with footage that used to only be taken from a manned helicopter. Drones in education are most commonly flying robotic vehicles that are used for this same purpose, photography. Most drones have four blades and these blades each have a motor attached to them. The four blades allow the drone to take off, land, rotate, spin, fly forwards and backwards, and maneuver into many different positions for your shots. The cost of drones can vary greatly based on the quality and features. Most have a camera that can be used for photos and video. Videos require more memory and optional storage cards can usually be added. We haven't tested many drones and can't make a list of recommendations but can offer some suggestions. Think about your purpose before deciding to buy a drone. For example, it will make a difference if you want to use it inside or outside. Inside there is little movement in the air, so a lighter and smaller drone might be fine. Outdoor use of a drone has more variables and a sturdier drone would be needed. Outside the drone can travel a greater distance. Many have features to automatically return the drone back to you and you will want this feature if the drone is going to travel far enough to be out of sight. We have found that it is best to purchase a drone where extra batteries and spare parts are readily available. Drone batteries are light so that they don't affect the flight of the drone and therefore don't last very long. You will want several batteries if you are buying a smaller, less expensive drone. Also, the motors can burn out and the blades can break so you will want access to replacement parts. You will want to vary the media in your posts and adding a drone to your equipment is an exciting way to get footage that will surprise your followers. Also, flying a drone and watching the camera on your smartphone screen is almost as much fun as driving a car for the first time! In 2007, Garnet Valley Elementary celebrated its ten year anniversary by having around 1,000 staff and students make the number ten on the football field. The original idea was for the local fire department to bring the hook and ladder truck to take a picture from high above the number formation. The truck ended up not being available so the picture was taken from the roof of the building. In 2017, for the twentieth anniversary, the picture will definitely be taken with a drone.

GoPro

GoPro cameras are small, durable, powerful cameras that are often worn on the body and used to record action sports. GoPro in education can be used to record the student experience. They can provide action shots during a physical education class, special event, or recess. They can also be used when shadowing students. The Shadow a Student Challenge, shadowastudent.org, is one example of an opportunity where school leaders or other educators can spend a day doing everything a student does from riding the bus, participating in class, and doing homework. This challenge is designed for educators to get the student's perspective and to be empathetic with the challenges a student faces each day. One way to share this experience with more people would be to use a GoPro to record events from the challenge. The video could then be edited and used to share the student's perspective with others like the school planning teams who are facilitating conversations about enhancing the student experience in our schools. A GoPro on a principal during a challenge like the dunk tank, a student/faculty basketball game, or other fundraiser would also provide plenty of entertainment and engagement on your posts.

Swivl

The Swivl robotic base holds your mobile device in place and tracks the speaker while recording. Initially used for flipping your classroom, the

Swivl will track you by a transmitter and also clearly record your audio. Swivl allows you to record videos yourself where you can move around and still stay in the shot. The Swivl base can spin around and also tilt up and down to track you. If you are making videos on your own, this robot can be very helpful.

Enhancing Photos and Video

Green Screen by Do Ink

A green screen is nothing more than a fabric backdrop or a color painted on a wall. When you record a video in front of a green screen, you can then use software to replace the green color in the background with an image. Green screen apps allow you to feel like a meteorologist on the evening news. This technology makes creating video a lot of fun. The Do Ink Green Screen app has three layers in the software. The first layer is for any animations that you want to add on top of the video and background image. The second layer is for the video, and the third layer is for the background image. You can now make videos with any background you'd like. Once exported, your video can be shared in your post to engage your followers with a video that can place you anywhere in the world. Garnet Valley Elementary has used Green Screen to make promotional videos to launch contests like the Winter Break Math Challenge where the school is divided into teams captained by the principal and assistant principal and the Spring Break Poetry Contest where winning students had their work highlighted on the school's Twitter feed.

Spark.Adobe.com

Adobe Spark is a free app that allows you to make professional-quality photos, videos, and stories for posting on social media. The app provides many templates and ideas. You can quickly use this site to create a graphic reminder for an upcoming event, add an image to a quote, or make a thank you card to post. School leaders don't have a budget for publicity so we do it on our own. Sites like Spark can help you create content that will make it look like you have a whole publicity team supporting you.

Panoramic Photos

iPhone users can take panoramic photos using the standard camera app. Special 360 degree cameras can also be purchased for the type of photo you would see on a real estate site with virtual tours of a home for sale. More simply, a panoramic photo taken with the iOS camera and posted directly on Facebook will give users a unique view. A globe icon will appear on the picture to indicate that it is panoramic and therefore has a wider view. When users click on the photo, they can move their device around and the view will move from side to side without them needing to use their finger to move the picture. The panoramic feature gives a sense of being there in person instead of viewing a photo. Panoramic views are ideal for photographing large events, events in wide open spaces with intriguing scenery, and events where many students are in the picture so that parents can rotate the view and look for their child. Panoramic photos enhance posts in your gym or auditorium for events like the school play or Jump Rope for Heart. They can also capture the enjoyment in students when the whole school starts the morning exercising together in the parking lot during ACES – All Children Exercise Simultaneously.

Filters, Effects, Stickers, Emoticons, and Collages

There are so many ways to jazz up your pictures before you post them. When posting multiple pictures, you'll want to use a collage app like Diptic or PicCollage. Collage apps allow you to join many pictures together, add borders and text, and put additional icons onto your pictures. Many collage apps along with some platforms will allow you to add special lens filters to change the appearance and mood of the photos. You can also add special effects, stickers like hats, glasses, or a mustache, and emoticons like smiling or laughing faces. All of these additions help to convey the feelings surrounding the event you are photographing and further engage your followers. Photo altering apps like Superphoto and Prisma let you transform your photos into popular works of art.

Create Your Own Content

Sometimes you can gain the attention of the user by creating eye-catching content. Online tools such as Canva, Pablo, Snappa, Recite, and Skitch are online graphic-design tools. Since tools are created and change frequently online, simply do a web search for free online graphic tools for social media. Create your content on the online program and publish it through your social media feed. Many programs have ways to send the content out directly through your social media platform.

Time Lapse Video

Another feature now built into the iOS camera is time lapse video. This feature takes several pictures over a period of time. The beauty of this native app is simplicity as the camera creates the video for you. Time lapse videos are ideal for items that move slowly over time, like a sunrise or sunset, where you can see the progression in one video that would be hard to notice in real time. Time lapse makes really cool videos in your Makerspace as well. As students design, explore, and create in your Makerspace, they can record their progress in time lapse to reflect on their progress. For more on Makerspaces, check out Laura Fleming's book, *Worlds of Making* (2015).

Increasing Interaction and Engagement

Tagging Others

Tagging other social media users in your posts alerts the users that you have mentioned them in your post. By tagging others, you can start a conversation. It also gives the tagged user a chance to Like, Share, Retweet, or Reply. Any time a public social media user chooses one of these options, their followers see the action that they took. This connects your post to more people than just your followers. In professional learning, we often tag authors of books we've read. A group of learners at Garnet Valley Elementary did a book share with leadership books. After one meeting, the group sent out three tweets about books they had read. The three tweets were then retweeted to over 207,000 people by the authors who were tagged in the posts. Additionally, one of the authors then offered to do a Google Hangout with the group during a subsequent meeting to discuss leadership in more depth. All of these connections were made via social media and professional learning.

BookSnaps

Tara Martin, @TaraMartinEDU, started #BookSnaps using social media to share artistically annotated photos of book excerpts. Challenges can be found on her @BooksSnapsREAL Twitter account. #BookSnaps are a fun, informative way to share what you are reading professionally and also to have students share an understanding of what they are reading. Since #BookSnaps are shared for others to see and interpret, they are a great way to interact with others through social media.

Blogs

Your social media journey will likely get to the point where you eventually have something more than 140 characters to say or you want to archive your thoughts in more than a Facebook post. This is when you are ready to start a blog. Like we suggested when first using social media, it is helpful to start by looking at and following other blogs. Starting your own blog is easy. There are free sites like WordPress, Weebly, Wix, or Blogger. You may also have a feature through your school website manager where you can host a blog about your school. Blogs are usually short, casual articles that are written on the blog and then shared through social media. Blogs can also start conversations and be interactive either through the comments section on the blog or by readers replying to the post on social media where you shared the link to the blog post. Blogs can also include pictures and videos. Blogs in education are often inspirational and thought-provoking when sharing ideas about teaching and learning.

KEY TIPS – Sites for Blogging

- WordPress – free to start with lots of themes and templates before upgrading
- Weebly – free and easy to use before going premium
- Wix – free or premium and used by beginners through businesses
- Blogger – always free and often used for personal use

Funny Videos

If you really want to get the attention of your followers, you have a few choices. One – win a really big award. Two – make a funny video about having no school on a snow day. Three – get your staff to lip sync in a video to a song like "Happy" or "Shake It Off." Take your pick. There are plenty of ideas on YouTube to get you started. Sometimes we just need to show our followers that we love our jobs and have fun doing them. No matter how good or bad your dance moves are, anyone can quickly embarrass themselves doing the "Whip/Nae Nae." Show that you have a sense of humor, attract some additional followers, and have a bigger audience to beam with pride when that award does come in.

Going Live!

The three major social media platforms that we use all now offer a "live" option. Live video on Facebook, Live on Instagram, and Periscope through Twitter can each be activated as one of the options when you start a new post. Once you activate the live video feed, the sites start to build viewers for you by notifying your followers that you are live. Once your live stream ends, look for options to post or save the video so anyone who didn't catch you live can still view it. Live video is really enthralling as you feel a rush of excitement about sharing what is happening in your school with raw emotion and feeling. Live options for awards ceremonies, spelling and geography bees, or quick updates are ways to connect with parents who are unable to make it in for special events. Announcing that you are going live also gets the students very excited as it makes each one of them feel like a celebrity who is being interviewed on the news.

Student Twitter Board

We first saw the idea of a student Twitter board at #NAESP16 in National Harbor during @TomMartellone's presentation. Tom talked about many ways to include student voice in his communication with parents. Twitter boards have since been launched in the schools of @Dr_Donnelly_WD and @JMKotchEdD. The boards offer students the opportunity to write a tweet that one of the principals can then tweet out from the school account.

Humans of New York (and Other Places)

Brandon Stanton started Humans of New York (humansofnewyork.com) as a photoblog, planning to photograph and interview 10,000 people in New York. The project expanded to a series of books as people were interviewed in many countries. Post are seen on Facebook by the 18 million people who have liked their page. This concept has been used in schools to learn about the people in our school communities. Humans of [insert your school here] can be posted on a blog or right onto your Facebook page. Your interviews probably won't fit in a tweet. Students conducting the interviews and writing the dialogue will be meeting English Language Arts standards in their work as your community comes together as little known facts about each other will be appreciated.

Digital Student Portfolios

ClassDojo (classdojo.com) and Seesaw (web.seesaw.me) are two sites and apps where students can upload their work to share with parents and be encouraged by their teachers and parents. These apps aren't used through your typical social media platforms but they are ways for your teachers to engage students and parents through digital media. Telling our stories is most successful when the stories are coming from many people and not just through the school leader. This is why Twitter is so important because you can easily connect with other educators in your school to like and retweet their content. Digital student portfolios share your school's story at a different and very important level. And, the more parents become comfortable with the expectations of connecting with your school then the more likely they will be to connect with you on social media as well.

Stories

Stories can be made on Facebook and Instagram. A story is a series of photos and videos that are linked together. The creator can also add text such as hashtags, social media handles, and links onto the photos and videos in the stories. Stories aren't seen in the timeline or news feed but are seen at the top of each app on a mobile device. A follower who clicks on a story sees more of your school's story as you can share multiple perspectives within the same post. It takes a little more time to make a story than to make a regular post with a simple photo, video, or collage but it also provides a different experience for your followers as we are trying to vary the media on our posts to keep increasing the engagement and interaction with them.

Tips and Tricks

If This Then That

IFTTT is an app that brings together applets and services. Applets are recipes that join together different services. IFTTT does the multitasking for you. It can automatically save your pictures, post from one platform to another, or update your profile picture any time you take a selfie. The applets are organized by the service that you use. IFTTT is helpful to keep your social media stream fresh as it can cross post on most platforms and update your users to your activity such as when you are going live. IFTTT is also helpful because it can archive your liked tweets, save your pictures, and create a spreadsheet of new followers. All of these things will come in handy when it's time to write your annual report or provide an update on your social media presence.

KEY TIPS – Useful Recipes on IFTTT

- Save the pictures from your posts to your Google Drive
- Update your profile picture
- Create lists of your followers
- Cross post on platforms
- Archive Facebook posts in a Google Doc
- Save the tweets you Like to a Google Doc

Business Tools

Social media sites are very intuitive as they generate revenue through advertisements and promoted posts. The site you use will realize that you are an organization and not an individual using the platform for personal reasons. You will receive alerts and notifications about using the business tools provided through the sites. The business tools will provide you with more analytical data about the performance of your posts and will also offer you the opportunity to make your posts more visible. Boosting a post can cost you only $5 and specials are occasionally offered so you can promote for free to see if you benefit from advertising. While schools don't need to advertise to generate business, sell products, or increase earnings, boosting a post can help to promote a special event that needs a lot of exposure to be successful. Schools can set a specific advertising budget to boost posts at different times while advertising for the event. Events that are open to the public are best to promote as paying for the advertisement will have users who do not follow you see the posts after they are carefully selected based on habits, followers, likes, and location. The sites will usually tell you how many followers the promoted post will go to before you make the decision to spend the money on publicity.

URL Shorteners – Bitly, TinyURL, bit.do

The URL is the internet address for a site where you want to direct your followers. Posting a link to a resource is the equivalent of adding an attachment to an email. If you are posting to promote an event or inform parents of a field trip that needs a permission slip, you can upload the forms on your website and then post the link on social media. The platforms will shorten the link or URL for you or you can use a URL shortening website. These sites take your long internet address and shorten it. So, when a follower clicks on the shorter link, the site directs them to the original address. The benefit of this is that your post looks cleaner and is shorter. A more easily remembered short URL is also easier to access later if the user is switching devices. The site bit.do allows you to customize your own link. The links start with bit.do/ and then you pick the final part. The site also tracks the statistics for you of how often the link was used. So, if you are planning a summer luncheon for new families who have recently moved into your school's attendance area, you can create a link such as bit.do/welcomenewfamilies that will take the parent to a registration form. The link is easy for parents to enter on any device. You can also compare the stats of how many times the link was used compared with how many people replied that they were attending. If the link has a lot of hits but not that many people are registered, it might hint that the details on the registration form didn't match their expectations. Maybe the date or time didn't work for the families' plans and now you know to make some changes for the next time.

Smore for Newsletters

A user-friendly and, even better, free online tool for newsletters is smore.com. There, principals can build newsletters that can be immediately published and shared via a simple link that is created once the page is populated and published. Different than the traditional newsletter, the online version allows for real-time edits and updates, which helps when calendars are adjusted and announcements have to be changed. With a few clicks, your newsletter can be easily updated and saved without having to print or resubmit. It is an easy way to connect your school's newsletter to various social media platforms, including your school's web page, as well as Twitter and Facebook. An example of the Puma Pride newsletter created on smore.com can be found through this link: www.smore.com/dvjbn.

Keep the list going! Connect with us on Twitter and Facebook, @7StepStories, and using #7StepStories. Share your own next steps as you try the ideas on the final to do list.

Step 7 – School Leaders To Do List

1. Connect with other school leaders to share, collaborate, and be inspired

2. Research and purchase a new device to create new media

3. Try different techniques for enhancing photos and videos

4. Create new content like blogs and #BookSnaps to increase interaction and engagement

5. Practice new tips and tricks to promote what is important to your story.

Concluding Thoughts

7 Steps to Sharing Your School's Story on Social Media began with setting the purpose for the work we do to connect with our community. As school leaders, we take the initiative to tweet and post because we believe that a strong connection between our schools and our community will increase student achievement and create an environment where everyone wants to learn and grow. There are many different types of schools in our world. Each school has its own personality, style, and place in the community. As we wrote this book, we thought and talked a lot about how schools, teaching, and learning have evolved.

Ten years ago we might have said that our schools should reflect our community. Now, we believe more than ever, that our schools challenge our communities to join with us in making the learning process one that is student-centered, innovative, inspirational, and powered by the limitless possibilities of technology. Our schools encourage students to ask questions, to learn through experience, to collaborate, and to go beyond what is expected. Sharing our stories is the connection that accelerates this mission. Before social media, the exciting news coming out of our schools was often delivered second-hand. Not any more! We now have the presence to write the narrative.

Every generation takes shape based on the experiences they have. What has changed in the world since you've been born that has affected your everyday life? Why wait for a generation to finish school before they begin to advance our progress? We are now instantaneous. We are now one with our students, parents, our community ... and our social media followers. Share your story because your story makes a difference, is influential, and will be positively contagious to those who listen.

Our schools encourage students to ask questions, to learn through experience, to collaborate, and to go beyond what is expected. #7StepStories

Many schools have become connected to each other and some are advanced beyond the point of calling social media an innovative practice in our schools. However, these 7 Steps are beyond just using social media to share a few lines and a picture. The plans we have shared are part of the process in creating a culture of innovation. The collaboration, critical thinking, perseverance, problem solving, and empathy that is fostered through this process adds to that culture. Setting a vision and goals that you aren't really sure you can achieve adds to that culture. Taking a risk to open your school's doors to the public adds to that culture. We don't take many of these steps alone. We celebrate the early adopters and just hope that a few more people join in to make a movement. When we see innovation, we want to tell everyone.

Your social media presence will expand your audience more than you could have imagined just a few years ago. Paper newsletter? We made one copy for each student and hoped for the best. Weekly email? We can monitor that and know that it is viewed a number of times equivalent to about 65% of our schools. Social media posting? 1,500 connections per post! 6,000 people per week! An increasing base that attracts 200 people more every year! So, what does it take to be inspired to share your story and build this culture?

We have been inspired in so many ways as we've gone down the path of using social media in our schools. We have been inspired by being connected educators and by other connected educators. We have been inspired by other authors who have taken their time to share their ideas with their readers. We have also been inspired by the connections we have made through our professional organizations and by the advocacy support that these organizations provide for us. And, ultimately, as school leaders we are continually inspired by our colleagues who contribute to educating our students each and every day. Without this inspiration, it would be harder to take as many risks, to be open to sharing so many ideas without knowing the response, or to find the extra time to look beyond the short-term objectives.

Becoming a connected educator was a quick journey for us as we both enjoyed using technology in our classrooms as teachers well before becoming administrators. There is something innate in us that attracts us to new ideas, gadgets, and ways of doing things. First joining Twitter, we started to read about education mostly from larger groups, media outlets, and organizations. The transformation to becoming connected came with attending conferences. Our shift actually took place in person.

In many schools, we were first instructed to keep our social media profiles private. We chose the highest security settings, maybe left out our last name, and didn't show any connections to our schools or districts. Then you get out of your safe space. You go somewhere like an EdCamp. You find hundreds of people doing the same thing you do. You are no longer one of five principals in your small, suburban school district or even one of forty in your county. You enter a conference, meet a few people, talk about staying in touch, and look for each other on Twitter. And then you realize you need to approve every follower. You realize that connections can't happen in real time because you can't keep up.

Next, you realize you have nothing to hide. That everyone you are interacting with has the same goals and a shared vision for pushing and supporting our schools to reach new heights. And so it happens. You get the feeling that YOU are going to be pushed and supported. You know that you are better because of the people you connect with, share ideas with, joke with, and mutually support. At that moment, you are no longer about you. You are now about others. You aren't learning to get recognized, to get a new job, or to be unique. You are connecting and learning to make everyone connected because you inspired them after being inspired by others.

And so it happens. You get the feeling that YOU are going to be pushed and supported. #7StepStories

We are connected with many individuals, groups, and organizations that we respect. All of these conversations are multi-directional. The leaders we connect with are just as good at listening as they are at talking and doing. They inspire us and are respectful of many social media norms. We connect through liking posts, retweeting, and mentioning when someone motivates us or compliments us. We stay connected after conferences and workshops by continuing to use the conference hashtag after the events have ended (see #EdCampLdr or #NPC17). Most of these connections are on Twitter but some also move to Facebook or Instagram as well. We also follow each other's schools as we build these connections. It is important for us to see all of our discussions at work as we motivate each other. Wherever you are with social media – a rookie, a dabbler, an occasional visitor, an early adopter, or a veteran – we hope that our 7 Steps provided you with some new ideas along with motivation and inspiration. Moving through these 7 Steps can go in order, start where you are, or jump around. The result of having the desire to share your stories and connect with us is all the same in the end. You've made it this far in the book and look at what you've accomplished!

Step 1 – Connecting Your Vision and Mission to a Social Media Purpose

We started by engaging our stakeholders in a strategic planning process to create a vision and mission unique to the school. From these statements, we developed a purpose for using social media. We live in an instantaneous society where social media delivers so much news. As school leaders, we want to be in that stream sharing the amazing events that occur in our schools each day.

Step 2 – Hashtag It

The hashtag (#) is the epitome of collaboration and connectedness. Creating a unique hashtag solidifies your school's place on social media and brings together users across platforms. Your hashtag can also become part of your identity as a school. Make it connect to your beliefs and watch it grow. From a yearly theme to the name of your PBIS program, your hashtag represents your school in many ways. After getting input from others in creating it, be sure to empower others to use it when they are posting.

Step 3 – Traditional Methods that Build a Social Media Following

Using social media is free (mostly) but promoting it won't be. You don't need to spend a lot of money but you will want to spend some. Alerting the students and parents in your school to your social media presence in traditional ways will connect with them where they are. So, make some postcards to give out at events, place magnets with your hashtag on cars, and design some cool t-shirts as giveaways. It might seem counterintuitive to promote your social media in places other than social media but it's a must to attract new users and followers.

Step 4 – Making It Happen

Schools are governed by boards who set policy and then led by admin-istrators who collaboratively set procedures and guidelines. As with any new initiative, be sure to start with reviewing any policies, procedures, and guidelines that will affect your plans. Once you are clear, it's time to set up your accounts. We provided a general overview of initial directions for using Twitter and Facebook to show you that it's not a lot of steps nor is it hard. There are many additional resources to help you such as tutorials on YouTube and also a lot of help and support through the platforms them-selves. You will also receive tips and advice through each platform once you set up your account. Start off with a goal whether it is one tweet per day or more. And, be sure to double your efforts by connecting Twitter to Facebook so that your posts move from one platform to another automat-ically. For your non-social media users, Storify is a powerful tool to share with them the story you are telling.

Step 5 – Will Anyone Follow Me?

Consistency is the key as we build our following of those interested in connecting with our schools. We post for different reasons. Our posts are informational, celebratory, and to increase engagement. To help be seen, we also educate our followers on notification and security settings. We make decisions about how to monitor followers and comments and also encourage more people to follow us by providing advance notification and news through social media before sharing through traditional methods like email and the website.

Step 6 – Is It Working?

You can view your success through resources built right into your social media platforms. Twitter Analytics and Facebook Insights provide many statistics for you to analyze and to guide your posting and storytelling. This information can identify the interests of your audience and also be used to encourage others to join you on social media when you share how many people are connecting with you.

Step 7 – What's Next?

Here's where we ask for your help and for you to join us in the adventure. "What's Next?" are ideas we have collected through connecting with others and trying to enhance our posts. You can connect with us on Twitter and Facebook (@7StepStories) to add more ideas to this list. We started with new techniques you can try now or come back and pick a new one when you are ready to mix it up a little. The categories are tools of the trade, enhancing photos and video, promoting interaction, and tips and tricks. We hope to hear from you!

After establishing your school accounts and building a base of follow-ers, it's time to get others moving too. We have been very intentional at building connected leaders in our schools. Connected leaders are con-nected educators who also help others to get started on social media. Connected leaders use social media to share stories and also for profes-sional learning.

Connected leaders are connected educators who also help others to get started on social media. #7StepStories

The #GVConnectedLeadership group has shared books like *Hacking Lead-ership* (Sanfelippo & Sinanis, 2016), *Kids Deserve It!* (Nesloney & Wel-come, 2016), *The Innovator's Mindset* (Couros, 2015), *Mindset* (Dweck, 2006), and *What Connected Educators Do Differently* (Whitaker, Zoul & Casas, 2015). The group met on several occasions to discuss and share ideas about professional learning and the use of social media. They dis-cussed mindsets, short- and long-term professional goals, and their book share outs. At the end of each meeting, the books were passed to dif-ferent people. Between the meetings, the readers posted #BookSnaps or replied to a question through Padlet.com. They also tweeted their favorite parts of the books and mentioned or tagged the authors. The first three tweets of this went to over 200,000 people! As the group continued, they talked about building and valuing your professional learning network or PLN. They even did a Google Hangout with superintendent and author, Joe Sanfelippo. Throughout the conversations, themes such as leadership, connections, growth, passion, learning, and opportunity were consistently heard. The members of this group continued their year using social media to tell stories from the classroom which opened up their doors to the many followers of the school account as well.

Being a connected educator opens the door to opportunities that you might not expect as your relationships build at many different levels. When a potentially valuable opportunity presents itself, you need to take full advantage of it. Being connected to local, state, and national organizations has brought together many connections for us. One of the most exciting opportunities we have had so far was to visit the United States Department of Education in Washington, D.C.

This experience never would have happened without our connecting through national conferences and with our professional organizations. We visited the Department through the Principals at Ed program where prac-ticing principals are brought into the Department for the day to learn about policy and to provide feedback on how policy influences decisions at the local level. We learned about the Every Student Succeeds Act and Title IIA and also wrote white papers to add to the Department's archives. The high-light of the trip was a roundtable discussion with then Secretary of Educa-tion, John King, who is the only Secretary of Education to have also been a principal. We talked about principal preparation and principal supervision along with sharing the problems of practice we had researched and written about in our white papers. Being two of the principals in the program and joining a dozen other principals from around the country was nothing short of amazing. And to think it all started at a conference, connecting through Twitter, and collaborating to enhance our schools.

While at the Department of Education, we pondered an interesting question, "What drives you?" We had to share our answer to this ques-tion during our introductions at the beginning of our visit. We still think about this question often as we stay grounded and focused on improving student achievement, promoting social emotional learning, and fostering innovative practices. So, if you are someone who is going to share your story on social media then what is it that drives you? It could be that you are proud of your school, that you want to engage more followers, that you want to collaborate with others to improve, or that you are invigorated by new trends. You might start sharing for any of those reasons or a combination of others.

There is one reason, though, that will drive you to keep going and to gain momentum. Sharing your school's story is a lot of fun! You will interact with more people, excite more students, develop more engaging lessons, have access to unimaginable resources and experiences, and lead a better school for our students. That is why we wrote this book. We are always trying new things, striving to enhance our craft, connecting with others, sharing and sharing more, and enjoying what we do. So, when an opportunity is there be sure to take it. Using social media to connect with students and families is an opportunity. Take it and make it amazing. Being a school leader isn't a job, it's a lifestyle. It's a force that is part of you in everything you do. Hopefully, the *7 Steps for Sharing Your School's Story on Social Media* have made online storytelling part of that lifestyle.

Writing our first book has been quite the experience as we have reflected on our practice, collaborated, and pushed each other to be better. Our hope for the future is that this book offers us the opportunity to connect with you through social media or in person. Just as technology is a vehicle to drive learning, we hope our 7 Steps fosters connections between our schools and yours and between us and you. There are many positive conversations about education going on through social media and we invite you to join ours. Connect with us on Twitter and Facebook using @7Step-Stories and #7StepStories. You've heard our story and how we got here and now we want to hear yours and learn from you.

References

Clemens Crossing Elementary School. (n.d.). About Us. Retrieved from http://cces.hcpss.org/about (accessed 6 May 2017).

Couros, G. (2015). *The Innovator's Mindset: Empower Learning, Unleash Talent, and Lead a Culture of Creativity*. San Diego, CA: Dave Burgess Consulting.

Dweck, C. (2006). *Mindset: The New Psychology of Success*. New York, NY: Random House.

Fleming, L. (2015). *Worlds of Making: Best Practices for Establishing a Makerspace for Your School*. Thousand Oaks, CA: Corwin.

Garnet Valley Elementary School. (n.d.). Connect with GVE. Retrieved from www.garnetvalleyschools.com/gves/connect (accessed 19 February 2017).

Garnet Valley Elementary School. (n.d.). Vision & Mission. Retrieved from www.garnetvalleyschools.com/Page/2838 (accessed 6 May 2017).

Howard County Public School System. (2013). Vision 2018. Retrieved from www.hcpss.org/vision/ (accessed 6 May 2017).

Howard County Public School System. (2016, June 9). Policy 8080: Responsible Use of Technology and Social Media. Retrieved from www.hcpss.org/f/board/policies/8080.pdf (accessed 6 May 2017).

Juliani, A.J. (2014). *Inquiry and Innovation in the Classroom: Using 20% Time, Genius Hour, and PBL to Drive Student Success*. New York, NY: Routledge.

National Policy Board for Educational Administration. (2015). Professional Standards for Educational Leaders. Retrieved from www.ccsso.org/Documents/2015/ProfessionalStandardsforEducationalLeaders2015forNPBEAFINAL.pdf (accessed 13 May 2017).

National Center for Missing & Exploited Children. (2017). NetSmartz Overview. Retrieved from https://www.netsmartz.org/Parents.

Nesloney, T. & Welcome, A. (2016). *Kids Deserve It!* San Diego, CA: Dave Burgess Consulting.

Sanfelippo, J. & Sinanis, T. (2016). *Hacking Leadership: 10 Ways Great Leaders Inspire Learning That Teachers, Students, and Parents Love*. Cleveland, OH: Times 10.

Sinek, S. (2013, September 29). Start with Why. Retrieved from www.youtube.com/watch?v=sioZd3AxmnE (accessed 18 February 2017).

Whitaker, T., Zoul, J., & Casas, J. (2015). *What Connected Educators Do Differently*. New York, NY: Routledge.